# Christology

# Christology
## True God, True Man

*Catholic Basics*
*A Pastoral Ministry Series*

Fr. Matthias Neuman, O.S.B.

Thomas P. Walters, Ph.D.
Series Editor

NATIONAL CONFERENCE FOR
CATECHETAL LEADERSHIP

LOYOLAPRESS.
3441 N. ASHLAND AVENUE
CHICAGO, ILLINOIS 60657

NIHIL OBSTAT: Rev. Daniel J. Mahan, S.T.B., S.T.L.
Censor Librorum

IMPRIMATUR: Rev. Msgr. Joseph F. Schaedel
Vicar General/Moderator of the Curia

Given at Indianapolis, Indiana, on February 19, 2001

The *nihil obstat* and *imprimatur* are official declarations that a book is free of doctrinal and moral error. No implication is contained herein that those who have granted the nihil obstat and imprimatur agree with the content, opinions, or statements expressed.

Acknowledgments appearing on pages 107–108 constitute a continuation of the copyright page.

Cover Design: Other Brother Design.
Cover Illustration: Steven Snodgrass
Interior Illustrations: Other Brother Design

**Library of Congress Cataloging-in-Publication Data**

Neuman, Matthias.
    Christology : true God, true man / Matthias Neuman.
        p. cm. – (Catholic basics)
    Rev. ed. of: True God, true man.
    Includes bibliographical references.
    ISBN 0-8294-1719-2
    1. Jesus Christ–Person and offices. 2. Pastoral theology–Catholic Church. I. Neuman, Matthias. True God, true man. II. Title. III. Series.

BT202 .N47 2001
232'.8–dc21                                                  2001029697
                                                                 CIP


ISBN: 0-8294-1719-2

Published by Loyola Press, 3441 N. Ashland Avenue, Chicago, Illinois 60657 U.S.A.
© 2002 The National Conference for Catechetical Leadership.

    07   08   09   Bang   9   8   7   6

# TABLE OF CONTENTS

# About the Series

**C**atholic Basics: A Pastoral Ministry Series offers an in-depth yet accessible understanding of the fundamentals of the Catholic faith for adults, both those preparing for lay ministry and those interested in the topics for their own personal growth. The series helps readers explore the Catholic tradition and apply what they have learned to their lives and ministry situations. Each title offers a reliable introduction to a specific topic and provides a foundational understanding of the concepts.

Each book in the series presents a Catholic understanding of its topic as found in Scripture and the teachings of the Church. Each of the authors has paid special attention to the documents of the Second Vatican Council and the *Catechism of the Catholic Church*, so that further learning can be guided by these core resources.

Chapters conclude with study questions that may be used for small group review or for individual reflection. Additionally, suggestions for further reading offer dependable guides for extra study.

The initiative of the National Conference of Catechetical Leadership led to the development of an earlier version of this series. The indispensable contribution of the series editor, Dr. Thomas Walters, helped ensure that the concepts and ideas presented here are easily accessible to a wide audience.

# Certification Standards: National Resources for Church Ministry

E ach book in this theology series relates to standards for theological competency identified in the resources listed below. Three national church ministry organizations provide standards for certification programs that serve their respective ministries. The standards were developed in collaboration with the United States Catholic Conference Commission on Certification and Accreditation. The fourth resource is the latest document, developed to identify common goals of the three sets of standards.

*Competency Based Certification Standards for Pastoral Ministers, Pastoral Associates and Parish Life Coordinators.* Chicago: National Association for Lay Ministry, Inc. (NALM), 1994.

These standards address three roles found in pastoral ministry settings in the United States. They were the earliest to receive approval from the United States Catholic Conference Commission on Certification and Accreditation. Copies are available from the National Association for Lay Ministry, 5420 S. Cornell, Chicago, IL 60615-5604.

*National Certification Standards for Professional Parish Directors of Religious Education.* Washington, DC: National Conference for Catechetical Leadership, 1998.

NCCL developed standards to foster appropriate initial education and formation, as well as continuing personal and professional development, of those who serve as directors of religious education (DREs). The standards address various areas of knowledge and abilities needed in the personal, theological, and professional aspects of the ministry. Also included is a code of ethics for professional catechetical leaders. Available from the National Conference of Catechetical Leadership, 3021 Fourth Street NE, Washington, DC 20017-1102.

*NFCYM Competency-Based Standards for the Coordinator of Youth Ministry*. Washington, DC: National Federation for Catholic Youth Ministry, 1996.

This document lays out the wide range of knowledge and skills that support ministry with young people, as well as the successful leadership and organization of youth ministry wherever it may be situated. The standards are available from the National Federation for Catholic Youth Ministry, 415 Michigan Avenue NE, Suite 40, Washington, DC 20017-1518.

Merkt, Joseph T., ed. *Common Formation Goals for Ministry*. A joint publication of NALM, NFCYM, and NCCL, 2000.

Rev. Joseph Merkt compared the documentation of standards cited by three national organizations serving pastoral, youth, and catechetical ministries. The resulting statement of common goals identifies common ground for those who prepare persons for ministry, as well as for the many who wear multiple hats. Copies are available from NALM, NCCL, or NFCYM.

# Introduction

The proclamation of any belief in Jesus Christ will not be an easy matter in this country of ours. A visitor to the United States who has little knowledge of Christianity would have a hard time figuring out exactly who Jesus Christ was—or is. The proliferation of "Christ images" in modern culture testifies to the pluralistic setting of American society. Catholics, Baptists, and Mormons offer various images of Jesus Christ, as do Jews and Muslims. Humanists, artists, commercial ads, and even MTV express still more contrasting images of this religious figure.

So then, who is Jesus Christ? He is Almighty God in human dress. He was a first-century sage preaching reverence of God and love for neighbor. He was an angel-like being with semidivine powers. He was a simplistic, religiously deluded individual crushed by Roman authorities. All these views—and more—were the grist for a cover article in the April 8, 1996, issue of *U.S. News & World Report*.[1] All these images of who Christ was, or is, are known to any reasonably well-informed resident of our country.

Because of the intense media-driven culture of American society, however, many people have a hard time differentiating between these images. They wonder which one is true. Often, their own views wind up a mixture of disparate elements. This struggle may even be the case with people raised in one particular Christian tradition. Chances are they have seen several contrasting images on television and in movies even before beginning formal religious education. This dilemma causes no small challenge for pastoral ministers, who must not only accurately convey the Catholic Church's teaching but also deal deftly with the myriad other images of Jesus Christ—and clearly show the difference.

To proclaim Christ today requires a variety of skills. Their purpose is to bring individuals to a clear knowledge of Jesus Christ and into a prayerful relationship with him. They help bring individuals into personal relationship with the living Christ; to make Jesus the example and guide of their lives; and to help them worship the living God through Christ and in the Spirit.

# To Know Christ Jesus

"I want to know Christ and the power of his resurrection and the sharing of his sufferings by becoming like him in his death. . . ." (Philippians 3:10). Saint Paul's words state the fundamental belief of the early Christian Church and the Catholic Church through the ages. The goal of faith is "to know Christ Jesus," who stands at the center of the Catholic Christian faith. The very name "Christian" means follower of Christ, disciple, believer in the Lord Jesus. Many other fundamental beliefs exist in Christianity (Trinity, Church, salvation), but all revolve around and receive their basic meaning from the belief in Jesus Christ.

This centrality of Christ shows in many ways throughout the Christian tradition. In the New Testament, the Letter to the Ephesians states, "Blessed be the God and Father of our Lord Jesus Christ, who has blessed us in Christ with every spiritual blessing in the heavenly places, just as he chose us in Christ before the foundation of the world to be holy and blameless before him in love" (1:3–4).

The same centrality permeates the creeds of the Church. The Nicene Creed proclaims: "We believe in one Lord, Jesus Christ, the only Son of God, eternally begotten of the Father. . . ." (*The Sacramentary*, p. 368). Likewise, in the devotional life of Christians, images of Jesus serve to powerfully orient people's response to God: the crucified Lord, the risen Savior, or the Sacred Heart. Finally, the *Catechism of the Catholic Church (CCC)* professes, "Moved by the grace of the Holy Spirit and drawn by the Father, we believe in Jesus and confess: 'You are the Christ, the Son of the Living God'.[2] On the rock of this faith confessed by Saint Peter, Christ built his Church.[3] Over time the

Catholic Christian tradition developed and expanded the basic belief in Jesus Christ into certain clear convictions. The study of this interrelated set of convictions about Jesus is called *Christology*. Christology does not merely look to the past. Like all parts of Catholic Christian belief, Christology grows and develops, continually clarified by faithful understanding. While reverencing past understandings of Christ, the Church of Jesus' followers seeks an ever-deeper grasp of his mystery and his relationship to our lives. Therefore, a full Christology includes acts of worship, devotion, and prayer to Jesus, as well as doctrinal understandings.

Although this book will focus exclusively on the Catholic Church's teaching on Jesus Christ, readers must not forget that this belief intersects with many other religious convictions. Some of these convictions are pivotal to Catholic faith (God, Church, sin, sacrament); others are of lesser stature (indulgences, purgatory, sacramentals). In addition, the belief in Jesus Christ can also become entwined with other areas of religious expression, such as the authority structures of the Church, devotional customs, or even personal goals. Sometimes, in an institution as large as the Catholic Church, the core issues can even become overshadowed by peripheral concerns. Thus, one ongoing aspect of Christian conversion seeks a return to the centrality of Jesus Christ in our daily living. Jesus announced clearly, "The time is fulfilled, and the kingdom of God has come near; repent, and believe in the good news" (Mark 1:15). The challenge stands ready; we must not only learn about Jesus Christ, but we must be willing to follow him wherever he may lead.

# The Catholic Christian Tradition

The particular understanding of Jesus Christ described in these pages will be that of the Catholic Christian tradition as embodied in the Roman Catholic Church. This tradition possesses a continuity reaching all the way back to Jesus and his first disciples. This

Christian tradition combines faith, reasoning, and history. All have a proper role to play in answering the question, Who is this Jesus?

The foundational document for Catholic Christian beliefs in Jesus Christ is the Holy Bible, the revealed books of the Old and New Testaments. We need to be very clear about this: Catholic faith in Christ finds its prime source in the Bible, especially the writings of the New Testament. But Catholic faith in Jesus Christ sees that biblical witness as embedded in the ongoing life of the Christian community, the Church. The Church reads and prays over sacred Scripture and draws out its meaning through the scope of history, prayerful worship, and critical thinking. This process, called *Tradition*, has played and continues to play a crucial role in the articulation of Catholic Christian belief in Jesus Christ through the centuries.

Tradition in this sense describes the ongoing life of the Christian community, led by God's Spirit, trying to be faithful to itself and the gift it has been given. The Second Vatican Council expressed this sense of tradition in *Dei Verbum (DV)*, (Constitution on Divine Revelation):

> Thus, the apostolic preaching, which is expressed in a special way in the inspired books, was to be preserved in a continuous line of succession until the end of time. . . . What was handed on by the apostles comprises everything that serves to make the People of God live their lives in holiness and increase their faith. In this way the Church, in her doctrine, life and worship, perpetuates and transmits to every generation all that she herself is, all that she believes. (#8)

A second, perhaps more common, sense of the word *tradition* might be more accurately called *traditions*. This expresses the specific and concrete ways the Church's faith in Jesus Christ gets formulated into language and communicated through the centuries. Among these specific instruments of tradition, first place must be given to the authoritative teaching of Church leaders (the magisterium) and, in particular, the doctrinal decisions of ecumenical councils and the authoritative teaching decrees of the popes. Other important instruments of tradition include the Church's worship and sacraments, the prayer and devotion of the saints, the ordinary catechizing in parishes, as well as the theological wisdom offered by Catholic thinkers. To arrive at a complete image of Jesus Christ, as seen in the faith of the Roman Catholic tradition, we must examine Scripture and tradition, history and faith, and theology and spirituality.

# Catholic Christian Faith in Jesus Christ—Major Points

Seven convictions capture the heart of Catholic faith in Jesus Christ. Each is treated in more detail in later chapters; the list below is a reference for future development.

1. The historical human reality of Jesus of Nazareth: Catholic Christology begins with an individual we can identify as one of us "who was descended from David according to the flesh . . . " (Romans 1:3). Jesus of Nazareth was born into a first-century Jewish culture on the far eastern edge of the expansive Roman Empire. He lived, carried out his religious mission, and died within that time.

2. The Resurrection of Jesus: After Jesus' tragic and violent death, something occurred that his disciples said had never happened before. The disciples believed and proclaimed that he was "raised" to a glorified life by the power of the God of Israel and exalted to a victorious union with God.

3. Incarnation: As the Church continued to live and pray the living mystery of Jesus Christ as truly "God with us," she came to confess him as the incredibly unique presence of God on earth. In Jesus, God became human like us, and in Jesus, the fullness of God's mystery is revealed.

4. The purpose of the Incarnation is for our salvation: The Church also came to believe that the reason for this incredible

divine action is found in the pure love of God for all humanity and creation. God desires "everyone to be saved and to come to the knowledge of the truth" *(1 Timothy 2:4)*. The will of God seeks to effect this purpose through Jesus Christ, who is our perfect mediator.

5. Jesus Christ as the fullness of true humanity: In Jesus, yet another factor is revealed: his life plunges us into the full mystery of our humanness, calling us to explore what it means to live a good human life in the most profound sense of the phrase. By looking at the life of Jesus, we learn to come to God.

6. The continuing presence of Jesus Christ among us now: Catholic Christians believe that Jesus has not left his followers to walk this earthly way alone and unaided. He continues to strengthen and grace those who believe in him with his unique sanctifying presence. This happens, above all, in the sacraments and in many other ways as well.

7. Jesus Christ as Lord of the Future: Finally, this Jesus Christ also directs creation to its true fulfillment. Whatever the Catholic faith says about death or judgment or heaven and hell is but a reflecting into the future of its belief in the mystery of Christ.

These convictions form the heart of a full Roman Catholic Christology. The key for any proclamation of the faith is the development of all of these beliefs in relation to one another. Together they become a Christology that provides a solid support for the other central beliefs of the Catholic tradition. In developing these seven convictions, this book offers a greater explanation of what the *General Directory for Catechesis (GDC)* affirms about proclaiming Jesus Christ.[4]

To carry out this plan, chapters 1 and 2 explore the Christological core of the New Testament. Chapter 3 traces the Church's belief in Christ from the apostolic era until the great ecumenical councils of the fourth and fifth centuries. Chapter 4 points out how the key issues of salvation and redemption in Jesus Christ continue to be refined and sharpened in the Church's belief. Chapter 5 looks at the influence of various images of Jesus in Catholic spiritualities through the ages. Chapter 6 explores the Catholic Church's belief that Christ's presence remains with us today, above all in the sacraments and personal prayer. And, finally, chapter 7 looks at a difficult contemporary problem: the relation of Jesus Christ to other religious saviors and world religions.

May these pages serve as an introduction to the Church's belief in Jesus Christ and spur a genuine conversion among readers to make Jesus more pivotal in their lives. The depth of a Christian's faith is still measured by that Christian's response to Jesus Christ's question, "But who do you say that I am?" (Mark 8:29).

# Summary

The Church's proclamation of Jesus Christ takes place in a modern cultural setting that presents many conflicting images of Jesus. Anyone who proclaims the faith must deal openly with this situation and endeavor to clearly affirm the belief of the Catholic Christian tradition, for Jesus Christ surely stands at the very center of Catholic Christian faith. Such has been the proclamation of the Church through the ages to the present. Thus, the goal of all catechesis becomes to know Christ Jesus in a faith-filled, loving relationship.

## ENDNOTES

1. "In Search of Jesus," *U.S. News and World Report* (8 April 1996).
2. *CCC* 424: *Mt* 16:16.
3. *CCC* 424: *Mt* 16:18; St. Leo the Great, *Sermo* 4, 3: PL 54, 150–152; 51, 1:PL 54, 308–309; 62, 2: PL 54, 350–351; 83, 3: PL 54, 431–432.
4. Especially "Jesus Christ: mediator and fullness of Revelation" (#40); "The object of catechesis: communion with Jesus Christ" (#80); and "The christocentricity of the Gospel message" (#98).

# FOR REFLECTION

1. What are some images of Christ in society that you as a pastoral minister will have to deal with?

2. In your own words, give a definition and brief description of Christology.

# CHAPTER 1

# The Witness of the New Testament

The whole New Testament witnesses to the mystery of Jesus Christ: who he was, what he accomplished, and what he continues to accomplish in the world and in people's lives. The New Testament confesses Jesus Christ as the one who sums up the whole history of God's dealings with Israel, who inaugurates the Church as the new community of God's people, and who begins a new and final chapter in God's dealings with creation and humanity, the definitive moment of God's revelation and plan. The Letter to the Colossians proclaims this belief. "He is the head of the body, the church; he is the beginning, the firstborn from the dead, so that he might come to have first place in everything. For in him all the fullness of God was pleased to dwell" (1:18–19). The *GDC* also summarizes this fundamental belief. "Jesus Christ is not merely the greatest of the prophets but is the eternal Son of God, made man. He is, therefore, the final event towards which all the events of salvation history converge [cf. Luke 24: 27]." (#40)

The New Testament writings, from the Gospel of Matthew to the Book of Revelation, express this centrality of Christ in a variety of ways. However, the Christian tradition has long given primacy of place to the four Gospels as the documents that most succinctly witness the mystery of Jesus in its full scope.

> The Gospels, which narrate the life of Jesus, are central to the catechetical message. They are themselves endowed with a "catechetical structure" [*Catechesi Tradendae On Catechesis in Our Time,* #11b]. They express the teaching that was proposed to the first Christian communities, and which also transmits the life of Jesus, his message, and his saving actions. In catechesis, "the four Gospels occupy a central place because Christ Jesus is their center" [*CCC,* #139]. (*GDC,* #98)

As a shorthand method of remembering, we might think of the Gospels as testifying to Jesus in three interrelated ways. These ways correspond to three structural parts of each of the Gospels. First, each Gospel begins with a faith statement of who Jesus really is in his truest identity (from Mark's baptism account to the stories of Jesus' miraculous birth in Matthew and Luke and, finally, to the hymn to the Eternal Word in the Gospel of John). Second, each Gospel presents an account of Jesus' ministry and teaching, his adult mission in life followed all the way from his baptism to his death on the cross. Third, each Gospel proclaims God's ultimate vindication of Jesus by raising him from the dead (the resurrection stories). The Incarnation of the Word, the ministry and death of Jesus of Nazareth, his resurrection, and the overarching conviction that all this is "for us and for our salvation" come together in a mix of faith and history that Christian believers describe as the "Christ-event," the beginning, heart, and end of their faith.

# Faith and History

Only a couple of decades ago, writing a life of Jesus Christ would have been a fairly straightforward endeavor in Catholic circles. The four Gospels of the New Testament provided the basic, factual, eyewitness accounts. One had merely to assemble these "facts" in a coherent narrative and fill in some relevant cultural and social history of the time—and there it was! Catholic bookshelves and parish libraries still contain many of these histories.

Alas, the task has become far more difficult today. The Gospels are no longer seen as simple factual historical accounts but as complex narratives of faith that weave together a variety of literary expressions. These might include testimonies of faith, moral encouragement, and historical recollection. Moreover, the final text of each of the Gospels results from an editing process that likely went on for several decades. These new perspectives actually give the Gospels a greater depth and complexity of meaning, but they also make the task of interpretation more difficult than before. The Second Vatican Council affirmed this basic view of all the biblical writings: "Rightly to understand what the sacred author wanted to affirm in his work, due attention must be paid both to the customary and characteristic patterns of perception, speech and narrative which prevailed at the age of the sacred writer, and to the conventions which the people of his time followed in their dealings with one another" (*DV*, #12). So, in interpreting a Gospel passage, what belongs to historical recollection and what to the testimony of faith?

Several other contemporary issues complicate our search for an outline of the historical life of Jesus. First, as the very structure of each Gospel implies, the "historical facts" of Jesus' life must be viewed in connection with two other equally important assertions: who Jesus really was and what he accomplished for us. The Gospel writers apparently preserved only those aspects of his life and work that "fit" with these two more important aspects. For example, several large segments of Jesus' life, like his adolescence and young adulthood, are mentioned only sparingly. What really mattered were his adult ministry, his teaching, and the ultimate giving up of his life for God's sake; these three aspects relate to the belief that he was the Son of God who came "for us and for our salvation."

A second factor that makes matters especially difficult today stems from the many other contemporary approaches to the life of Jesus. Fundamentalist and evangelical Christians, for example, take everything in the Gospels as literal and historical fact. They make much of labeling those who disagree with them as "not really Christian." On the other hand, rigorous and critical historians who write scholarly biographies of Jesus omit anything hinting of the supernatural; they fill in the gaps extensively with cultural material of that time, all of which seems to have great "scientific veracity." Groups like the Jesus Seminar have received much publicity by loudly announcing "shocking reversals" of ancient beliefs and presenting Jesus in terms that almost invade people's cherished notions.[1] Another contemporary group consists of all those who provide "visions"—as in *The Poem of the Man-God*[2]—that profess to give an exact account of everything Jesus said and did. Teachings, sayings, and events that have nothing to do with the Gospels are said to have been revealed through modern visions or locutions. These claims can be particularly insidious because they appear to be pious and devout. Presenting a view of the life of Jesus within a Roman Catholic Christology requires clearly drawn lines of difference between the many divergent expressions.

The position on "faith and history" taken here will be that recommended by the International Theological Commission's *Select Questions on Christology (SQC)*.

> Jesus Christ, the object-referent of the Church's faith . . . is a man who lived in a concrete milieu, and who died after having lived his own life within the unfolding of an historical process. It follows that historical research concerning Jesus Christ is demanded by the Christian faith itself. . . . [and] within the boundaries proper to exegetical research, it is certainly legitimate to reconstruct a purely historical image of Jesus. . . . The substantive and radical unity between the Jesus of history and the glorified Christ pertains to the very essence of the Gospel message. (#I.A.1, 1.2, I.B.2.2)

History is one (necessary) component of Catholic faith, but it is not the sole determinant. The "historical Jesus," or what we can know of Jesus' life, activities, and teaching on purely historical grounds, must be balanced with the faith perspectives of the living Church tradition.

Four topics form the framework for all Christology: Incarnation of the Word; the ministry and death of Jesus of Nazareth; his Resurrection; and the saving work of Christ. These topics structure the outline for chapters 1 through 4.

The treatment of these themes begins with the Resurrection. Chronologically, that shattering, marvelous event first revealed God's total acceptance and exaltation of Jesus and his ministry. That conviction of faith then spurred the apostles to a deeper reflection on Jesus' life, ministry, and death, as well as a reflection on his true identity.

# The Mystery of the Resurrection

The death of Jesus did not end his life story or his influence over his followers. Saint Peter's sermon, related in the Acts of the Apostles, affirms, "This Jesus God raised up, and of that all of us are witnesses" (2:32). To Jesus' disciples, however, the Resurrection and Jesus' subsequent appearances initially came as a sudden, unexpected, and even shocking event: "While they were talking about this, Jesus himself stood among them and said to them, 'Peace be with you.' They were startled and terrified, and thought that they were seeing a ghost" (Luke 24:36–37). Yet, in a powerful act of faith, the disciples believed that Jesus lived in a new, transformed, glorified way, raised up by the power of God and exalted to the right hand of the Father.

Belief in the Resurrection of Jesus forms the absolute basis of Christian faith, both in its beginning and in its ongoing life. But, and this point must be clear, the term *resurrection* not only refers to a real historical event upon Jesus, but it also describes a profound and complex series of faith convictions that shape an entire way of looking at reality. The Resurrection shapes the Christian's very way of believing.

In the last fifty years scholars have been restoring the event of resurrection faith to its central and rightful place in Christian belief. The resurrection faith defines the origin, core, and exemplar of what it means to be a Christian. What makes us Christians? Ultimately, that we believe God raised Jesus from death to life and in that action created a new religious vision and bestowed a new divine power in all creation. "The Paschal Mystery has two aspects: by his death, Christ liberates us from sin; by his Resurrection, he opens for us the way to a new life" (*CCC*, #654). The real power of faith in the Resurrection, however, lies not in the fanciful events that people often imagine. The stories of the appearances, the reaction of the women and the apostles, and the conversations between Jesus and others are, in fact, narratives that encase powerful convictions and commitments. The resurrection narratives exemplify a Gospel story that has been shaped to carry within it an absolute conviction.

In its quality as a narrative, a story brings a great personal immediacy to the presentation, but the deep faith convictions hold much more power. These faith convictions proclaim what Jesus accomplished by his death, the newly understood meaning of existence and human life, and God's will for all people. Taken together, the resurrection accounts express a vision and a hope for which the followers of Jesus were actually willing to die. These powerful faith convictions emerge in the themes that run through the accounts of Jesus' appearances to his followers. The following paragraphs summarize these themes.

The Resurrection of Jesus names a totally new act of the God of Israel. The real emphasis in resurrection should not be placed on the revivified body of Jesus, but on God's resurrecting action! The very same God who brought the Israelites out of Egypt, who gave them the Torah on Sinai, and who led them back from Exile performed yet another great and definitive action—the raising of Jesus to a glorified life at the right hand of God. "But God raised him up, having freed him from death . . ." (Acts 2:24). This act of God occurred as a real event in our world at the end of Jesus' human life, but it reverberates through all time and space. Such a completely unexpected action of the God whom Jesus called "Father" would compel Jesus' disciples to rethink absolutely everything about him.

Resurrection asserts that Jesus now lives in an entirely new and glorified mode of existence. The Jesus who lived, preached, and died in Judea is the same Jesus raised to life by the power of God stretching into human history. "Although the Resurrection was an historical event that could be verified by the sign of the empty tomb and by the reality of the apostles' encounters with the risen Christ, still it remains at the very heart of the mystery of faith as something that transcends and surpasses history" (*CCC*, #647).

Jesus has passed beyond our world to the very right hand of God. This divine act vindicated the whole life and work of Jesus. All that Jesus did and taught must now be reevaluated by his followers as leading up to this new revelation of God. His cross shows that a holy life can be liable to great suffering; yet, in that suffering and death the possibility of new life for all creation is revealed.

This resurrecting act of God has resulted in the beginning of a new stage in human history and creation. Those who believe in Jesus will also be transformed (changed) by the same power—God the Father—that transformed (raised) him. The appearance accounts exemplify this theme in a number of ways. Jesus' followers were welded into a holy community, working toward the same resurrected transformation by living as Jesus did (see Luke 24:48–49). Believers were commissioned to preach the good news of God's new act, to carry the hope of transformation to all people. "Go therefore and make disciples of all nations. . . ." (Matthew 28:19). And the presence of the Spirit in our hearts carries God's promise and pledge that this larger resurrection still goes on.

All these points can be compacted into a single and unitary belief of resurrection faith, which is the heart and soul of Christianity. One who believes the resurrection faith is convinced that God's action really happens in the world, that it happened in Jesus' Resurrection as the prime exemplar, and that it still happens where people come together in true, sharing community, where the Spirit gives increased insight into the meaning of life and where an act of loving service becomes a remembering witness of God and Jesus Christ. God's action happens in a way that says that the end of God's act is still hidden, and so in this life we encounter God only in a limited way, "through a glass darkly" (see 1 Corinthians 13:12). To live the Resurrection means to always seek opportunities to increase our love and hope.

The whole complex of events (the Passion, death, Resurrection, Ascension of Christ, and the bestowal of the Spirit) is often referred to as the paschal mystery. Its grand and special celebration occurs during the yearly feasts of Holy Week and Easter, but it also forms the central meaning of each Sunday's celebration of the Eucharist. "Jesus rose from the dead 'on the first day of the week.'[3] . . . For Christians it has become the first of all days, the first of all feasts, the Lord's Day . . . Sunday" (*CCC*, #2174).

To believe that God has raised Jesus means to accept a "new birth into a living hope. . . ." (1 Peter 1:3). This hope looks not just to the distant future; it affects the way we understand our human reality, relate to others, and live here and now. Our belief in resurrection calls forth from us, fundamentally, a practical hope that can challenge the threats and despair of modern life. Christians, as all people, know too well the many disappointments and failures that the course of life brings. But they also believe in a religious strength that helps them press on, and in a religious courage that impels them to find meaning and love once again—until they are overtaken by the infinite love of God and drawn as closely as possible to this saving God. The challenge for Catholic Christians today is to affirm and exemplify this hopeful conviction. We need to let our "living hope" shine through in our work, play, worship, and relationships; in building communities of peace and love; and in valuing every human being as a child of God destined for a glorified, divine life.

In summary, the Resurrection was and remains many things: a unique act of God, an event in the life of Jesus, and the exemplar of the transforming experience at the core of Christian faith. Resurrection remains the central event in the development of the Church's Christology. It stimulated and continues to stimulate an ever-deepening vision of who Jesus was in his life history and who he is in his deepest reality.

# The Divinity of Jesus

As the followers of Jesus probed more deeply the implications of the Resurrection, it became evident that Jesus had been more than just a human being—even an extraordinary human being— raised by God; his was a closer relationship to God than the disciples ever imagined.

The beginnings of this faithful quest into the identity of Jesus can be glimpsed in the New Testament writings themselves. They initiate a search that will not be concluded until the final formation of the Nicene Creed at the ecumenical council of Constantinople in 381. That creed professes clearly, "[O]ne Lord, Jesus Christ, the only son of God, eternally begotten of the Father . . . true God from true God . . . one in Being with the Father" (*The Sacramentary*, p. 368).

The Christian community in those first years after Jesus' death struggled over how to express this wild and almost unthinkable assertion—and it would take hundreds of years to attain a satisfying expression. The difficulty of the task should not be underestimated. Even though the Church eventually arrived at a clear statement of the divinity of Jesus Christ, there were disagreements, inadequate expressions, and hesitations along the way. It must be remembered that Christians of Jewish background were struggling to say what had never been said before in the Jewish tradition. At the same time, other Christians of a Greco-Roman background were trying to formulate the same belief in a manner that would clearly separate their Christian belief from those of the traditional Greek and Roman myths. (This might help people today be more understanding of efforts to express the same belief in a twenty-first-century culture.) Here we shall briefly show the beginnings of this effort as reflected in the New Testament. Chapter 3 takes up the story in subsequent centuries of early Church history.

Some New Testament writings show clearly that they already considered Jesus Christ in a way that far exceeded any model known in ancient Judaism (e.g., prophet, king, or Messiah). Consider the Letter to the Colossians:

> *He is the image of the invisible God, the firstborn of all creation; for in him all things in heaven and on earth were created, things visible and invisible, whether thrones or dominions or rulers or powers—all things have been created through him and for him. He himself is before all things, and in him all things hold together. He is the head of the body, the church; he is the beginning, the firstborn from the dead, so that he might come to have first place*

*in everything. For in him all the fullness of God was pleased to dwell, and through him God was pleased to reconcile to himself all things, whether on earth or in heaven, by making peace through the blood of his cross.* (1:15–20)

In this passage, and others like it, Jesus possesses divine characteristics and performs actions traditionally reserved for God alone (creation, forgiveness of sins). Note that God-language was used much more loosely in the first-century Roman Empire than in today's world. Use of such language makes it difficult to interpret exactly many New Testament passages. Still, we can glimpse a number of ways that the followers of Jesus were coming to believe in him in an ever-closer connection to the very mystery of God.

The first way of showing the divinity of Jesus was to bestow on him various titles, like Son of God, Incarnate Word, or Lord. New Testament writers did this in profusion. A proper title carries an indication of the person's identity and the standing that person possesses in relation to others. A study of the titles for Jesus found in the New Testament uncovers a rich mine of Christological thought.

"Son of God," for example, counts as one of the most significant titles given to Jesus throughout the New Testament. Even though in many passages it carries no overtones of divinity, there are other texts in which it definitely conveys a unique sense of divinity in Jesus. After the Resurrection, Jesus' followers would move clearly in this latter direction. The very beginning of Mark's Gospel affirms, "The beginning of the good news of Jesus Christ, the Son of God" (1:1). And again, at the end of the Gospel, the centurion proclaims, "Truly this man was God's Son!" (15:39). At the beginning of Luke's Gospel the angel announces to Mary, "[T]herefore the child to be born will be holy; he will be called Son of God" (1:35). The key notion in Jesus' Sonship describes his relationship with God as completely different from that of any other human being. His Sonship was not given or bestowed but flowed from the very core of his being, a divine filial relationship.

Another popular and powerful title given to Jesus was "Lord" (*Kyrios* in Greek). This title too, attested to a growing belief in the divinity present in Jesus. Like "Son of God," "Lord" can mean various things. It can be a simple title of address; it can refer to one who is highly exalted; and it can be a specific signification of divinity. A clear example of the latter use occurs in the famous hymn from the Letter to the Philippians.

> Therefore God also highly exalted him
>> and gave him the name
>> that is above every name,
> so that at the name of Jesus
>> every knee should bend,
>> in heaven and on earth and under the earth,
> and every tongue should confess
>> that Jesus Christ is Lord,
>> to the glory of God the Father.
>
> (2:9–11)

Another passage appears in Paul's First Letter to the Corinthians. "[Y]et for us there is one God, the Father, from whom are all things and for whom we exist, and one Lord, Jesus Christ, through whom are all things and through whom we exist" *(8:6).* Paul has taken the classic Jewish confession of one God *(see Deuteronomy 6:4–5)* and woven Jesus Christ into it, giving him the title "Lord," which usually referred to the unique God of Israel. Calling Jesus "Lord" again draws a connection to divinity by making Jesus share in God's dominion over all things.

It might be valuable to say a brief word about the title "Christ." Originally, it was a proper title bestowed on Jesus to indicate that he was the "Anointed One," who would free Israel from all foreign oppressors. Very quickly, however, this title seems to have been judged inadequate to express all that Jesus' followers wanted to affirm about him. Thus it gradually became a part of his regular name: Jesus Christ.

A second way the early Christians expressed their belief in the divinity of the risen Jesus was to assign to him particular actions that had previously been attributed to God alone. These included knowing and revealing God, changing the divine law, forgiving sins, reconciling people to God, and being the agent for God's final kingdom. The passages quoted above from the Letter to the Colossians (1:15–20) and 1 Corinthians (8:6) clearly see Jesus as the agent of creation, as the power that holds all things in existence, as the fullness of God's presence on earth, and as the reconciler between God and the human race.

A further use of this attribution to Jesus of God's ancient prerogatives was the role of the risen Jesus in bringing about "the Day of the Lord." That phrase signified the belief of the ancient prophets of Israel that a time would come in the future when God would intervene decisively in the world. This intervention would judge the wicked, restore the land and people of Israel, and manifest God's glory in a dazzling final victory. New Testament writers saw the risen Jesus as the one who would fully accomplish this consummation of all things. "He will also strengthen you to the end, so that you may be blameless on the day of our Lord Jesus Christ" (1 Corinthians 1:8).

Clearly, some Christians were already thinking of Jesus Christ as being divine or God-like in a very real way during the New Testament period (ca. A.D. 30–100). Their assertions may not have the technical clarity of later Church councils, but they provide a real step in that direction. By the end of the New Testament period, Jesus even seems to be spoken of, at least occasionally, as "God." We see such attribution in the first chapter of John's Gospel, probably written toward the end of the first century… "In the beginning was the Word, and the Word was with God, and the Word was God" (1:1). At the end of John's Gospel, the apostle Thomas addresses the risen Jesus directly, "My Lord and my God!" (20:28).

As Christians pushed their belief ever deeper in a confession of Jesus' divinity, two related beliefs began to appear. First, to acknowledge Jesus as God demands some expansion of the traditional notion of one God. Accordingly, the relationship between Jesus and God became Son and Father (and later Spirit) in one God. Christology leads directly to Trinity. In their *Theology*

*Christology Anthropology (TCA)*, the International Theological Commission makes this point explicitly. "Christian theism consists properly in the triune God, and he is known uniquely in the revelation to us in Jesus Christ. Thus . . . knowledge of Jesus Christ leads to a knowledge of the Trinity and attains its plenitude in the knowledge of the Trinity" (#I.B.1.2). But it will take time—centuries—for the full implications to be worked out.

The second belief affirms that in a very real way Jesus Christ was a new revelation of God. As much as human beings can know God—for Catholic Christians the context of that knowing comes not from cultural or supposed ideas of God, but from the concrete life of Jesus of Nazareth. Whatever might initially be thought about the justice, anger, or wrath of God, all must be reevaluated in the light of what we know and believe about Jesus. In his service, love, and compassion—in his total humanity—Jesus reveals to us the fullest face of God as we can know it.

To that humanity we now turn.

## SUMMARY

The New Testament first and foremost bears witness to the mystery of Jesus Christ. The Gospels are primary sources for our knowledge about Jesus Christ as well as the affirmation of the Church's faith in him. To know the Gospels, Catholic Christology recognizes the importance of merging faith and history. These same factors interact in clarifying and expressing the Church's belief in Jesus Christ. Jesus' humanity is known and studied by history; his Resurrection, divinity, and saving work are confessed by faith. Jesus' Resurrection caused his disciples to see his earthly ministry in a new way; his was a closer relationship to God than they had ever thought. Jesus' Resurrection and the struggle of his disciples to express that faith also gave a unique shape to the message they would proclaim to others. In Jesus, God acted anew to create a new relationship between God and humanity.

## ENDNOTES

1.  "In Search of Jesus," *U.S. News and World Report* (8 April 1996).
2.  Maria Valtorta, *The Poem of the Man-God* (Isola dell' Liri, Italy: Centro Ed. Valtortiana, 1986).
3.  *CCC* 2174: Cf. *Mt* 28:1; *Mk* 16:2; *Lk* 24:1; *Jn* 20:1.

## FOR REFLECTION

1.  How would a Catholic Christian evaluation of the Gospels differ from that of a fundamentalist Christian?

2.  Why was it difficult for the first Christians to even imagine the divinity of Jesus? Could these difficulties still be problems for people today?

3.  Name some practical ways in which the living hope of the Resurrection might be expressed in real-life circumstances today?

CHAPTER 2

# Seeking the Life History of Jesus

Catholic Christian faith believes in the full humanity of Jesus Christ. Even though some Catholics today have a tendency to think of Jesus as the Son of God, or simply as God, the great Catholic tradition recognizes the importance of his actual human life for faith and theology. The Apostles' Creed outlines a simple life trajectory: "Born of the Virgin Mary, suffered under Pontius Pilate, was crucified, died and was buried." We all share that human journey: we are born, we suffer, we die.

A full human life, however, encompasses much more than that, and many believers desire to know a more personal Jesus. They want to know him as a Jew in his specific Jewish setting, a real human being who lived in a specific place, time, and culture. *Gaudium et Spes (GS)*, "Pastoral Constitution on the Church in the Modern World," of the Second Vatican Council states this desire beautifully. "For, by his incarnation, he, the son of God, has in a certain way united himself with each man. He worked with human hands, he thought with a human mind. He acted with a human will, and with a human heart he loved" (#22).

Indeed, every authentic Catholic Christology emphasizes and meditates on certain aspects of Jesus' humanity as part of the full Christ-mystery. Devotional expressions can easily get off track if they are not continually checked by going back to the historical life of Jesus. Reflection on Jesus' human journey forms in us the basis of an active and profound faith. The Letter to the Hebrews does not hesitate to call Jesus "the pioneer and perfecter of our faith" (12:2). In coming to know the humanity of Jesus, we discover the full value of a human life (and our lives), of one love (and the loves in our lives), and the value of a vocation (and the callings of each of us). We do not forget the divinity of Jesus but use his humanness as an essential stepping-stone to make that act of faith in the mystery of his being Immanuel (God-with-us). Sometimes we have to know Jesus Christ in the same way as did his first disciples and apostles: to know him first as teacher and master, then as the power of God in him and, finally, as the very mystery of God Incarnate. Let us then consider what we know of the life of this remarkable individual.

The previous chapter notes that the four Gospels of the New Testament are the main source of our knowledge about the actual life of Jesus. Outside of the New Testament, and in other books of the ancient world, a few tidbits can be found, but they offer no significant expansion. So, we return again and again to those four writings. Our first task will be to know exactly what kind of writing they are; such knowledge will provide some guidelines to the kind of information we can expect to find in these Gospels. (At this point it would be helpful for readers to review *DV*, chapter 3.)

A "gospel" should not be understood as a biography in the modern sense of that word—as an accurate factual presentation. Rather, the Gospels are "good news," presenting the life and mission of Jesus to inspire and nurture our faith in him. Moreover, that life and mission are augmented in the light of what God did for him (the Resurrection) and who he was (the Son of God). Often in the Gospel narratives these latter two points are written back into the remembered deeds and sayings of Jesus. In that way, reading a Gospel bears a resemblance to looking at a photograph composed of three simultaneously exposed images; it takes some effort to separate what belongs to Jesus' historical ministry, to the proclamation of the Resurrection, and to the naming of his true identity. Today's biblical scholars must face this task. The Catholic Church accepts this challenge. The International Theological Commission of the Catholic Church notes clearly: "Jesus Christ, the object-referent of the Church's faith . . . is a man who lived in a concrete milieu, and who died after having lived his own life within the unfolding of an historical process. It follows that historical research concerning Jesus Christ is demanded by the Christian faith itself" (*SQC*, #1).

In addition, the Gospels most likely went through several stages of development. First, there were some remembered words and deeds from Jesus' human life. Second came the telling and development of those stories as remembered by the first Christian communities. These people applied the stories to their own time and situation and wrote those insights into the original story of Jesus, for they believed he was still present with them guiding them as risen Lord. Finally, a single writer collected these community stories and put them together into the final text of the Gospel that we have today.

This threefold development has been affirmed by the Biblical Commission of the Catholic Church. "In order to determine correctly the trustworthiness of what is transmitted in the Gospels, the interpreter must take careful note of the three stages of tradition by which the teaching and life of Jesus came down to us" ("Sancta Mater Ecclesia," as quoted in Neuner and Dupuis, *The Christian Faith [CF]*, p. 90).

The stories of Jesus' birth (the "infancy narratives") are a major section of the Gospels affected by this new perspective. In the writing style of the time, these stories stated clearly "who Jesus was" in comparisons that would have been readily understandable to the people of the first century. In his book titled *The Birth of the Messiah: A Commentary on the Infancy Narratives in Matthew and Luke*, Catholic Scripture scholar Fr. Raymond Brown summarizes:

> Close analysis of the infancy narratives makes it unlikely that either [Matthew or Luke] . . . is completely historical. . . . The common instinct to draw so heavily upon the Scriptures [the Old Testament] suggests that for each evangelist the infancy narrative was to supply a transition from the Old Testament to the Gospel—the Christological preaching of the Church presented in the imagery of Israel (p. 36–37).

This does not mean that these stories should not be read and loved at Christmastime; they should be. The crucial point to remember is that they make their strongest point about the true identity of Jesus far more than simply recounting the events of his birth.

In the end, a life history of Jesus may only identify sketches or vignettes of his adult life, but nothing approaching a complete life history. "A 'biography' of Jesus in the modern sense of this word cannot be produced, if it were taken to entail a precise and detailed account" (*SQC*, #I.A.1.1).

The vision of the life and ministry of Jesus that we will endeavor to outline from the Gospels will be only a series of topics and events that can be identified using the criteria of strict contemporary historical investigation. Only a partial picture emerges, yet one that retains an immense value. Even though the Resurrection culminates the life and ministry of Jesus, and eventually leads to a confession of his unique relationship to God, we should not forget all that leads up to it: the life, ministry, and death of an individual man, Jesus of Nazareth. The historical human reality of Jesus Christ forms an essential part of an integral Roman Catholic Christology.

# The Major Events of Jesus' Life

As a prelude to a richer understanding of Jesus in his life setting, some reading in the Judaism of his time is appropriate. Knowledge of the religious culture of first-century Judaism adds to an understanding of the life history of Jesus. "During the greater part of his life Jesus shared the condition of the vast majority of human beings: a daily life spent without evident greatness, a life of manual labor. His religious life was that of a Jew obedient to the law of God, a life in the community" (*CCC*, #531).

Even a survey of this topic is beyond our scope here, but serious believers should not neglect it.

## THE BAPTISM

Although little definite information is known of Jesus' life before he was baptized by John in the Jordan, that event remains one of the surest historical facts from the earliest Christian tradition. All the Gospels present the baptism as the beginning of his public ministry (his own ministry). In receiving John's baptism he accepted a call from God to become a proclaimer of God's message, a traveling preacher in Israel, moving from town to town and proclaiming the spiritual renewal and purification of Israel.

He was not alone in this task; we know from other documents of the time that many itinerant teachers took up a similar mission.

The accounts of Jesus' baptism also tell of his awareness of a unique relationship with the God of Israel. This is told in the tradition of God's voice: "You are my Son, the Beloved; with you I am well pleased" (Mark 1:11). Here stands a key moment of Jesus' filial awareness of having a special and unique relationship with the God of Israel. Perhaps also hidden in this account is a summons to accept the task (vocation) of the suffering servant of Isaiah (see Isaiah 42:1), to share in and prefigure the destiny of the whole people. The faith affirmations of later Christian generations also abound in these stories, but the core of an actual historical event lies at their base.

## THE TEMPTATIONS

The temptation accounts demonstrate in a particular way the full humanness of Jesus. They were not just a show of power to manifest his divinity. Rather, the Gospels see them as real temptations to be struggled against. They indicate real battles of will against challenges to Jesus' chosen vocation. The Gospel accounts place the temptations immediately after Jesus' acceptance of his mission (in Baptism), but it seems likely that they are compacted accounts that summarize what Jesus had to face throughout his entire life. The passage "When the devil had finished every test, he departed from him [Jesus] until an opportune time" (Luke 4:13) suggests as much.

Biblical scholars wonder about the exact content of the temptations and the alternatives Jesus faced. Because the Gospel writers parallel Jesus' temptations in the light of the great temptations of the people of Israel, this concern cannot be addressed easily. The temptation accounts, as we now have them, are drawn to show the fulfillment of Israel's history in the life of Jesus. Tempting Jesus to turn stones to bread recalls the people demanding bread in the wilderness (see Exodus 16); the temptation to throw himself down from the Temple and trust in angels echoes the rejection of the responsibilities of the covenant and reliance on an unrealistic trust in God (see Exodus 19); the temptation to bow down and worship Satan resembles worshiping the golden calf (see Exodus 32).

Whatever their exact content, the temptation accounts affirm the real struggles Jesus endured to faithfully live out his chosen vocation. Israel in the desert succumbed to these temptations, but Jesus stood steadfast to the end.

## PROCLAIMING THE KINGDOM OF GOD

One theme dominates the human life of Jesus and his ministry to the people of Israel: his proclamation of the kingdom of God. The summary of his entire message, given by the evangelists at the beginning of Jesus public ministry, states boldly: "The time is fulfilled and the kingdom of God has come near; repent, and believe in the good news" (Mark 1:14; see Matthew 4:12–17 and Luke 4:14–15). Proclaiming God's kingdom was central to Jesus' mission in life, and he became a powerful teacher of that kingdom. His parables, miracles, and symbolic gestures point toward understanding and realizing the kingdom of God. At times both followers and opponents called him "teacher" or "rabbone," a form of address that indicated one who has taken up the task of preaching spiritual renewal and who has been approved by God and the people.

What exactly does that phrase "the kingdom of God" mean? (Similar expressions are "kingdom of heaven" and "reign of God.") Biblical scholars most often describe it as a common Jewish phrase to express God's active role in people's lives. God's "kingdom" happens where and when God's love, justice, peace, and communion really dominate people's thoughts and actions. Jesus seeks to make that begin right here and now.

"Kingdom" does not primarily denote a place but an action or an event that happens to people. "Kingdom" functions as a symbol for God's rule exercising itself over people and people freely responding to it. We ought to think of the kingdom of God more as a dynamic action rather than as a set and fixed reality of any kind. In the midst of the wide range of first-century

Jewish hopes and theories about where and how one meets God, Jesus proclaimed his teaching on the kingdom: the experience of God happens now in a person's life. Jesus said, "The time is fulfilled!" The changing power of God stands ready here and now. The experience of God happens to ordinary people in the everyday circumstances of their lives.

## In Parables

A key aspect of Jesus' ministry was his proclamation of the kingdom in parables. "With many such parables he spoke the word to them, as they were able to hear it; he did not speak to them except in parables, but he explained everything in private to his disciples" (Mark 4:33–34).

We often look at what Jesus said—but just as important is how he said it. Parables constitute a special style of teaching common to the first-century Jewish world, one frequently used to make a point in a certain way. Today, parables are somewhat distant from our world. We should have a clear understanding of how a parable operates, however, if we are to grasp one of the most profound aspects of Jesus' life and ministry.

In the last twenty years a great deal of attention has been given to the scholarly study of Jesus' parables and the nature of the parable in general. Parables function like poetic metaphors. Some metaphors work as direct illustrations: "My feelings were a raging bull!" Most people are familiar with these metaphors and use them all the time. But other kinds of metaphors function as "participative narratives," and they may be unfamiliar to modern ears. In these participative metaphors, a sudden reversal of image or meaning initiates (startles) the hearers into a new way of looking at things. In so doing hearers are exposed to a "different world."

Parables as participative metaphors evoke a new reality that intrudes into ordinary and usual perceptions. Images like "a terrible beauty" or an "aching love" challenge people to a complex new way of seeing the world. Sometimes a participative narrative may shock people into hearing the experience from the inside, a move that merges feelings people seldom associate with one another.

Jesus' parables are like great poetry. They begin in common human experience—what everybody assumes to be true—and then explode those assumptions. Hearers are challenged to a new way of perceiving things; that's the dynamic of a parable. The parables of Jesus shattered many commonly accepted views of the first-century Jewish world about God and God's relations with people. Jesus' parables can still surprise modern hearers into perceiving and accepting the kingdom of God in their lives.

For example, Jesus' parables enter into the discussion—frequent and raging during his time—of "where" one meets God. To those who said that God will come in the future, Jesus said, "From the fig tree learn its lesson. . . ." (Mark 13:28). To those who maintained that God transcends all and must be worshiped only in the highest heaven, Jesus replied, "The kingdom of God is as if someone would scatter seed on the ground. . . ." (Mark 4:26); "The kingdom of heaven is like yeast that a woman took and mixed in with three measures of flour. . . ." (Matthew 13:33).

The parable is just told; the hearers must grapple with the veiled meaning. Consider a parable that still bothers many people: the story of the owner of a vineyard who hires workers at the third, sixth, ninth, and eleventh hours (see Matthew 20:1–16). Those who have worked the longest expect more and are shocked when all receive the same payment. Jesus' hearers are left to grapple with the notion that God's mercy and justice operate differently from human standards of justice and mercy.

## HIS HEALING MINISTRY

For the Gospel writers, one of Jesus' major activities was his healing ministry. The writers recount wonderful deeds happening throughout his life: curing the sick, casting out demons, raising dead people to life, even demonstrating control over the forces of nature. Jesus specifically connected these healing events, especially the casting out of demons, to his proclaiming the kingdom of God. "But if it is by the Spirit of God that I cast out demons, then the kingdom of God has come to you" (Matthew 12:28).

Whereas many modern scholars do not accept the historical veracity of some of Jesus' miracles—in particular the nature miracles—practically all agree that Jesus was a public healer of many ills and that he healed in a way that was considered remarkable by his contemporaries. Jesus connected the source of these healing actions to his teaching on the presence and power of God in human life. A healing is a sign that the presence and power of God is present and operative.

Jesus' healing ministry witnessed God's salvation extended to the total person, including the spirit and body. All aspects of our lives need to be healed. The healings called for faith on the part of the one healed or on the part of family and friends. This separated Jesus from other miracle workers in Jewish and Greek traditions. In the case of the woman with a hemorrhage we hear, "Daughter, your faith has made you well. . . ." (Mark 5:34); in the case of the blind man from Jericho, we hear, "Go; your faith has made you well" (Mark 10:52). These are almost as much faith stories as healing stories.

The Gospel healings convey another powerful aspect of Jesus' life: his compassion. Human suffering and illness touched Jesus deeply. He cried at the death of Lazarus, for example; and he was profoundly moved by the widow of Naim. That compassion shown by Jesus showed was the very compassion of God flowing through him to human lives. To practice compassion still remains one of the greatest of healings, even in today's age of psychological awareness, Jesus shows us that any true compassion mirrors the heart of God.

## THE DISCIPLES

The Gospel tradition unanimously affirms that Jesus gathered a group of disciples around him. The disciples were distinct from the general supporters who followed and accepted his teaching. A common custom of the Jewish culture of Jesus' time saw a teacher gathering pupils and followers, but Jesus' callings show certain distinctive differences. Jewish teachers accepted disciples who first came to them, but Jesus called his disciples directly and individually. For example, "As Jesus passed along the Sea of Galilee, he saw Simon and his brother Andrew casting a net into the sea—for they were fishermen. And Jesus said to them, 'Follow me and I will make you fish for people'" (Mark 1:16–17). In addition, Jesus demanded a complete and immediate response from the one who was called. The disciple-to-be must enter into a total relationship with Jesus; the only response could be to join him wholeheartedly in his mission—which meant giving up a great deal. "Another of his disciples said to him, 'Lord, first let me go and bury my father.' But Jesus said to him, 'Follow me, and let the dead bury their own dead'" (Matthew 8:21–22).

Jesus' call conveyed a brand new and profoundly radical meaning to a person's life. Discipleship involved a lifetime following, and it included suffering (see Matthew 10:34; Luke 9:59–62 and 14:26). Jesus' disciples would share in his own work to become fishers of men and women, to help people realize, respond to, and love the transforming presence of God in their lives. Jesus deliberately sought to form a small group into a force that would continue spreading his mission of proclaiming the kingdom of God. The group's key purpose would be to continue Jesus' work, to teach and minister the God-experience in people's lives, that all might enter into an increasingly fulfilling and life-sustaining relationship with the heavenly Father. Such a relationship brought to followers the peace and hope that gives direction and encouragement amid the struggles of daily living (see Matthew 10:9–13). Jesus confirmed his followers in this charge by sharing a last meal with them before his death.

## THE PASSION AND DEATH OF JESUS

The final and the most important events of Jesus' life history came with his passion and death. These historical facts, above all others, gave witness to his full humanity. The fact of his death remains about as historically certain as anything could be. But few accompanying details of those last hours can be certified with much reliability. All the Passion narratives in the Gospels have been formed and shaped by theological interests of later writers. The brutal and shameful death of Jesus constituted an embarrassment and challenge to his followers, even as they believed in his resurrection. Why did it have to happen this way? All the Passion accounts are concerned primarily with providing a response to that shattering question.

We may detect the events of Jesus' last days only in shadowy outline. 1) There was some kind of scene when he entered the city (the "palm" procession). 2) An incident in the Temple (the "cleansing") aroused much anger among his opponents. 3) Jesus celebrated a famous memorial meal with his disciples (the Last Supper). 4) Jesus was betrayed by one of his own disciples (Judas). 5) The events of the trial remain extremely confused and many versions have been constructed from the Passion accounts.[1]

The bald facts of crucifixion and death, however, cannot be dismissed; they remain very important in Christology. A growing agreement among scholars asserts both Jesus' knowledge of his approaching death and his willing acceptance of this death as part of the realization of God's kingdom. "Truly I tell you, I will never again drink of the fruit of the vine until that day when I drink it new in the kingdom of God" (Mark 14:25).

For Catholic theology the important fact remains that Jesus willingly accepted his death as part of his obedience to God and the consequence of fidelity to God's message. The International Theological Commission asserts that, for Catholic faith, Jesus' death is the "willed consequence of the obedience and love of Jesus making a gift of himself." This is "a complex act, at once active and passive (Galatians 1:4; 2:20)" (*SQC*, #IV.B.2.2). Jesus, in faith, died for the salvation of those who believed in him. This act of self-giving summed up his whole life and mission.

In sum, therefore, we do not possess sufficient material for a complete biography of Jesus in the modern sense. But enough historical material exists to draw a picture of a human being with a powerful religious message about God, one who taught and healed and chose disciples to carry on his message. He also pursued that mission with great fidelity, even to the point of giving up his life. However, after his death events were to prove to his disciples that he was much more than that.

# Jesus' Life Events as Mysteries

The knowledge of a precise understanding of Jesus' life, teaching, and actions is important beyond the perspective of historical inquiry. When brought into conjunction with the faith affirmations of the Resurrection and the divinity of Jesus discussed in the first chapter, these life events become genuine "mysteries of faith." All that he did and said takes on a profound value in light of God's actions toward us and our reaching toward God. The *CCC* captures both of these faith directions.

> Christ's whole earthly life—his words and deeds, his silences and sufferings, indeed his manner of being and speaking—is Revelation of the Father. (#516)

> In all his life Jesus presents himself as our model. He is "the perfect man,"[2] who invites us to become his disciples and follow him. In humbling himself, he has given us an example to imitate. (#520)

Notice the two ways in which the facts of Jesus' life become mysteries: they reveal something of God and God's attitude toward us, and they reveal our human way toward God. The New Testament affirms that Jesus reveals God the Father: "'Whoever has seen me has seen the Father'" (John 14:9), and "He is the image of the invisible God, the firstborn of all creation. . . ." (Colossians 1:15). Christians need to take these sayings seriously; Jesus' attitude toward sinners says more about how God sees the sinner than do all the systems of justice and punishment derived from human investigations and experience; Jesus called disciples and taught us that God always invites and beckons people to conversion of life.

In a second faith direction, humanity becomes the "way" into understanding Jesus' divinity and the meaning of the kingdom of

God. Christian followers of Jesus who believe him to be ultimately significant in their relationship with God should seek to live the life he lived. Believers are challenged to live those same life events and mysteries of Jesus' life transposed into their own life settings. Jesus proclaimed that the kingdom of God constitutes, in this moment, a source of human strength. We might ask ourselves, How forceful are we in saying that a response to God should be a part of everyone's life?

In seeing the events of Jesus' life in this way, the humanity of Jesus becomes a special and unique way to God. The International Theological Commission identifies precisely this as a reason for seeking a sound historical knowledge of the life of Jesus: "to afford a better perception of the place occupied in the salvation of mankind by the humanity of Christ and by the various "mysteries" of his life on earth, such as his baptism, his temptations, and the "agony" of Gethsemani" (*SQC*, #II.C.7).

The *CCC* does not hesitate to speak in this way of some of the more difficult moments of Jesus' life: the temptations, the social conflict, his physical sufferings, and the moment of abandonment by God (see #538–540, 603, 612). All of these mirror our lives and our hopeful ways to God.

Many Christians, as part of their real faith commitment, live some aspect of the life history of Jesus in the contemporary world: preaching the good news of God's kingdom, caring for the sick, engaging in a ministry to the grieving and dying, providing help to the poor, setting an example of prayer, and so on. Each person gives concrete witness to the full humanity of Jesus Christ. An accurate study of the life events of Jesus should always look to this further goal, to assist and deepen the faithful in truly imitating the life of Jesus.

# Summary

A Catholic Christology affirms the full humanity of Jesus Christ and uses modern historical tools to gain as accurate a picture as possible. The basic information about Jesus' life comes from the four Gospels of the New Testament. It is crucial to know what kind of documents these Gospels are and the information to be derived from them. Certain major events in Jesus' life are historically grounded: his baptism, the temptations, his proclamation of the kingdom of God, his healing ministry, and his passion and death. Joining this life history to the singular event and faith-affirmation of the Resurrection, a further Christological step sees them as "mysteries" of Christ's life. Both reveal God to us and show us the way into our true humanity.

### ENDNOTES

1. One point that historical scholarship has recently clarified, and which Church authorities have quickly responded to, is the responsibility and culpability of the Jewish people in the death of Jesus. Historical research places much more blame on Roman officials and soldiers. One must be very sensitive to the possibility of anti-Jewish attitudes arising from a cursory reading of the Passion narratives.
2. *CCC* 520: *GS* 38; cf. *Rom* 15:5; *Phil* 2:5.

# For Reflection

1. Can you think of an image that would help people understand the overlapping information about Jesus in the Gospels?

2. Identify one story in Jesus' life and rewrite it for today's world. Then make connections back to the original story.

3. Choose an event of Jesus' life history and explain its aspect of "revealing God" as well as its aspect of revealing our true humanity.

# CHAPTER 3

# Christology and the First Ecumenical Councils

After the end of the New Testament period (roughly the year A.D.100), Christianity continued to spread throughout the Roman Empire and beyond. Small communities of Christians began to appear in all major cities and in far-flung rural areas. They all believed in Jesus Christ and spread the message about the Galilean teacher who was truly God Incarnate. A typical example of this clearly accepted belief in Jesus Christ comes from a letter of Ignatius, a bishop of Antioch (in modern-day Lebanon), written most likely in the first decade of the second century. "Under the Divine dispensation, Jesus Christ our God was conceived by Mary of the seed of David and of the Spirit of God; He was born, and He submitted to baptism, so that by His Passion He might sanctify water" ("To the Ephesians," #18).

This faith received from the tradition of the apostles spread through the steady growth of the Christian movement.

# Confusion About Christ

Problems began to develop, however, among these widespread groups, problems that would eventually cause great changes both in the unity of the Christian communities and in how they expressed their belief in Jesus Christ. The first problem was simply lack of communication or frequent contact. Distance and long periods of isolation meant that some Christian groups could and did develop quite distinct expressions of belief, customs of life, and forms of worship.

The second problem fed off the first and arose from the diversity of cultures, philosophies, and other religions that Christians encountered throughout the far reaches of the Roman Empire. For example, challenges caused by meeting a particular "opponent" would cause one group of Christians to develop and accentuate an aspect of their own life and belief that other Christians might not stress. These imbalances caused uncertainty and tensions whenever the various Christian groups did get together.

The third problem that tied into both previously mentioned difficulties occurred when converts to the Christian faith imported aspects of another religion or philosophy into their Christian practice. Such integration could begin to cloud the expressions of faith received from the early Christian community. In fact, this problem did occur not only with secondary issues but also with the very faith in Jesus Christ. For example, sharp disagreements erupted over his real nature and identity as well as how he saved us. Each of these groups, however, considered themselves to be Christians, true followers of Jesus Christ. Sometimes any number of these diverse groups of Christians could be found together in the same large city. Most of the Christian groups in the following discussion appeared during the second century.

Some Christians retained strong ties to their Jewish roots. They continued to practice many Jewish religious customs (the observance of Torah, the practice of circumcision, and the observance of traditional Jewish fasts, for example). They believed in Jesus, but they understood him within the framework of the traditional Jewish affirmation of only one God. They did not like the extravagant (as they saw it) affirmation of Jesus as God in some of the New Testament writings. They believed Jesus to be a "prophet," the greatest of prophets, the Messiah of Judaism. To these Jewish Christians, Jesus remained completely human, without virginal conception and without any hint of divinity.

Opposed to these Jewish Christians were those whose beliefs stemmed from the teaching and leadership of a man called Marcion. They were sometimes called Marcionite Christians. Marcion lived in the middle of the second century and came from Sinope in Pontus, a region in Asia Minor (modern-day Turkey), where his father was bishop. His perspective rejected anything with Jewish roots, especially the sacred writings of the Jews. He held basically to the Christianity expressed in the letters of Saint Paul and not much else. To him, the God of the Jewish covenant was a God of wrath, whereas Jesus proclaimed a different God of love. Marcion believed Jesus Christ was God

Incarnate, but he wasn't sure if Jesus was really and truly human. Jesus revealed the new Christian God of love.

Still another faction was the Gnostic Christian community that emphasized "*gnosis*," or a special revealed knowledge. These small gatherings of Christians modeled themselves after philosophical "study groups" of Greek and Roman philosophers but with Christian teachers as guides. In all likelihood, many of the Gnostic Christian teachers had belonged to Greek, Jewish, and other forms of gnosticism before becoming Christian. Gnosticism spread far and wide in the Roman Empire. Its characteristic blending of many aspects from different religious traditions (Judaism, mystery religions, Greek pantheism) created a multitude of gnostic beliefs. In their eclectic manner, they resembled the New Age movement of the twentieth century. Christian Gnostics wove aspects of Christianity into this religio-philosophical mix and changed Christian faith in the process. They saw Jesus Christ as a spiritual "principle" that existed between God and the world. Jesus wasn't really a human being, and most Gnostic Christians did not believe that he really died on the cross. Instead, he was to them a kind of semidivine revealer who brought the true, hidden knowledge about God, the world, and human beings. Gnostics, above all, claimed gnosis, a secret knowledge that showed the true way to heavenly salvation.

# A Catholic Church Tradition

In addition to the previously named Christian groups, others considered themselves faithful to the tradition received from the apostles. They believed in a united worldwide (catholic) expression of faith continuously handed on from the earliest years of the Church. They called themselves "apostolic," or "Catholic Christians." The growing differences between the various Christian factions made these Catholic Christians aware of the necessity to establish some marks of identification, some way of clearly recognizing that traditional faith handed down from the apostles. The great achievement of Catholic Christians over the next one hundred and fifty years (ca. 150–300) was to establish a Church tradition that would consolidate, remember, and hand on that apostolic faith. Four basic pillars formed the supports of their Christian tradition.

First, Catholic Christians eventually agreed on a canon, a list of sacred books that became the Christian testament: the "New" Testament. Achieving a commonly accepted list was a lengthy process, taking almost two hundred years (ca. 180–367). A second pillar was the formulation of a creed, a short summary listing beliefs that all the Catholic Christian churches adhered to. Public sacred actions (the sacraments) formed a third pillar as the manifest worship and prayer of Catholic Christians. The fourth and last foundation stone of this Church tradition emerged as a stable leadership: a college of bishops.

This effort to establish a Church tradition counts as a great moment in Catholic Christian Church history. This tradition identified a common basis to which Catholic Christians could always return for a clear grounding in the Christian faith they pursued. Catholic Christianity announced a public and historical faith, not hidden truths as in Gnostic Christianity. In addition, Catholic Christianity embraced a universal and worldwide vision, unlike separatist and elitist Christian groups like the Marcionites. The Catholic Christian group called themselves the "Great Church" (one, holy, catholic, apostolic). For them, the gathered bishops were leaders who succeeded the first apostles and decided the parameters for true Christian life and faith. The Scriptures (especially the New Testament), the beliefs expressed in the creed, the Church at worship, and the leadership decisions of the bishops: these four pillars were then—and remain now—the ongoing tradition of Catholic Christianity.

The development of these four pillars notwithstanding, Catholic Christians still were forced to deal with the other views about Jesus Christ. To this end their leaders the bishops met together in councils and considered the Bible, the creeds, the worship of the people, and the insights of theologians. They then articulated the faith of their Christian tradition. In the second and third centuries these meetings first took place at the regional level, but in the fourth century, events occurred that caused the introduction of a new and broader system: the "ecumenical" council. This council involved all the bishops of the Catholic Christian Church. The first ecumenical councils addressed several areas concerning belief in Jesus Christ. Their decisions shaped the Church's basic doctrinal tradition, a tradition still observed today.

## The Ecumenical Councils

When the formation of the Catholic Tradition took place (ca. 150–300), another development was creating a stir throughout the Christian world. Some Christian thinkers attempted to express the universality of Jesus Christ and his salvation in ways that would be more understandable to minds cultivated in a Greco-Roman culture very different from the Jewish milieu in which Jesus had lived. The general culture of the Roman Empire had been strongly shaped by the traditions of Greek philosophy, especially that of Platonism and Stoicism. Thus, the proclamation about Jesus Christ to people of that culture needed expression within the context of the words, meanings, and vision of the Greco-Roman world. This first process of "inculturation" would ultimately find success, but it would also lead to major developments in the understanding of Jesus Christ among the Christians themselves.

One of the most momentous steps happened when several major Christian thinkers, especially Saint Justin Martyr, began to speak and write about Jesus Christ as the *Logos*, or Word, of God. The Gospel of John in the New Testament used this word frequently, but Justin took another step and developed the notion of Logos within the understandings of Greek philosophy. In that setting, Logos could mean many things: "word," "meaning," the all-pervading "principle of rationality," and the "basic order of the world." By calling Jesus the "Logos of God," Justin asserted that what happened in Jesus Christ affected the entire makeup of all creation, and, therefore, Jesus' saving work was truly universal. For the Greeks, universality constituted almost a must for any idea to have lasting validity. Justin wrote in a famous treatise: "We have been taught that Christ is the first-born of God, and we have declared above that he is the Word (Logos) of whom every race of men were partakers; and all those who lived with reason are Christians" ("Apology," 1.46).

Gradually "God's Word," "God's Reason," and "God's Order of Creation" became the privileged ways that Greek Christians thought about Jesus Christ. What really happened in Jesus was God's Logos entering into human history and changing the "order and meaning" of everything.

This crucial step in Christian thinking held both good news and bad news for the future of Christian belief and practice. The good news announced that Jesus Christ could indeed be preached and believed in as the universal Savior of the world. The bad news, however, was that the exact relationship of the Logos to God as Supreme Creator and Father remained unclear, because in Greek philosophy the Logos was "lesser than" the One or Supreme Principle of all things. As a result, Christians began to entertain conflicting views of Jesus as the Word of God. Some saw him as equal to the Father; others judged him as below the Father and created by the Father. These clashing views eventually came into public conflict, and the first ecumenical councils would have to address the conflict.

Another fact contributing to the emergence of the ecumenical councils may be found in the changed destiny of the Christian Church in the Roman Empire during the first decades of the fourth century (especially from 312–325). In 313 the Roman emperor Constantine made Catholic Christianity a legal religion and began to show it great favor and protection. Soon the Christian Church became such an important social force in the entire Roman Empire that the bishops needed a clear, unified statement of belief, purpose, and practice. A meeting of all the bishops, representing all Christians, could make such a statement.

The controversy over the identity of Jesus Christ erupted in 318 with a dispute in the city of Alexandria (Egypt) between two Christian factions. One, headed by a notable presbyter named Arius, held that the Logos in Jesus "was not, before he was begotten, or created. . . . The Son had a beginning, but God is without beginning" (Stevenson, *A New Eusebius: Documents Illustrative of the History of the Church to* A.D. *337*, p. 325). The other faction, headed by the Bishop Alexander and a deacon named Athanasius, held that the Word in Jesus was fully divine and that when people prayed to Jesus Christ they were truly praying to the one eternal God. Bishop Alexander believed that the Logos in Jesus Christ was on the same level as the Father; the Logos is, therefore, fully God. To Alexander this belief represented the faith of the Church in prayer and worship: To meet Jesus Christ is to meet God. The dispute soon spread from the city of Alexandria to most of the eastern half of the Roman Empire. The Christian Church found itself openly divided on a matter of the greatest urgency.

To resolve the dispute Emperor Constantine called a "worldwide" (or ecumenical) council of bishops to meet at the city of Nicaea (near Istanbul in what is now Turkey). This meeting became the first ecumenical council of the Catholic Church. Council decisions, like those of later ecumenical councils to the Second Vatican Council of the twentieth century, became an essential foundation stone of the Church tradition for all Catholic Christians. The bishops at the Council of Nicaea heard both sides of the argument, debated the issue, and overwhelmingly voted for the position of Bishop Alexander and the deacon Athanasius.

To promulgate their decision to all the Catholic Christian Church, the bishops issued a new creedal statement for the universal Church. Catholic Christians still recite this Nicene Creed every Sunday at Mass. The text of this creed would not receive its final formulation, however, until the next ecumenical council of Constantinople in 381. That later council added specific statements about the divinity of the Holy Spirit and the Spirit's distinctive work in the Church and the world. The Nicene Creed states of Jesus Christ:

> We believe. . . in one Lord Jesus Christ, the Son of God, the only-begotten generated from the Father, *that is, from the being of the Father, God from God, Light from Light, true God from true God, begotten, not made, one in being with the Father,* through whom all things were made, those in heaven and those on earth. For us men and for our salvation He came down, and became flesh, was made man, suffered, and rose again on the third day. He ascended to the heavens and shall come again to judge the living and the dead.
>
> (*CF*, p. 6)[1]

In the end, the Council of Nicaea proclaimed that Catholic Christians profess Jesus Christ as truly and fully divine, "Son of God" in the most fundamental and real sense of that phrase. To pray to Christ and adore Christ is to pray to and adore God. Still, it took over fifty years for the decisions of Nicaea to be accepted by most of the main body of Catholic Christians. The full implications of that belief remained to be worked out in an understanding of God as Trinity. Indeed, the proclamation of the Logos as divine established a key step leading to an expanded understanding of God as Triune Father, Son, and Holy Spirit.

Several decades after the furor of Nicaea ended, another question about Jesus Christ again divided Christians into several opposing parties. Since the divinity of Christ had been clearly established by the first two ecumenical councils, Christian thinkers began to explore his humanity. To what extent and depth can he still be said to be human like us? Some theologians began to maintain that Jesus had a body like ours, but not a human mind capable of willful and, therefore, sinful decisions. They wanted to absolutely ensure the sinlessness of Jesus. Other Christian thinkers objected, saying that it was necessary for Jesus to be a complete human being, with a real human body, mind, and soul like ours—otherwise the human mind would not have been saved by Jesus' incarnation. This complicated religious dispute embattled Christians for almost a century. The differences again caused great division between groups of Christians.

Finally, the ecumenical council of Chalcedon in 451, called by the Emperor Marcion, achieved another fundamental decision for Catholic Christians, this one about the relation of the human and the divine in Jesus Christ. That council, too, issued a formal statement of belief.

> [W]e unanimously teach to confess one and the same Son, our Lord Jesus Christ, the same perfect in divinity and perfect in humanity, the same truly God and truly man composed of rational soul and body; the same one in being with the Father as to the divinity and one in being with us as to the humanity, like unto us in all things but sin. We confess that one and the same Lord Jesus Christ, the only begotten Son, must be acknowledged in two natures; without confusion or change, without division or separation.
>
> (*CF*, p. 66)

Chalcedon not only achieved the confession of both full humanity and divinity in Jesus Christ but also established a basic set of terms to be used in a technical explanation of who Jesus Christ is. In Christ, two "natures" (divine and human) exist together in one person (a single existent reality). The practical effect of this distinction meant that the Catholic Church fully accepted the complete humanity (human nature) of Jesus. Moreover, the bishops at Chalcedon affirmed that in the union of the divine nature and the human nature no mixing or obliteration of either occurred. This ensured that people would not conclude that the divine nature blotted out or completely controlled the human nature. The International Theological Commission explains the point further. "'Without confusion' obviously refers to the two natures, and asserts that the humanity of Jesus is an authentic one. . . . 'Without division' proclaims the very deep and irreversible union of God and man in the person of the Word. God's full immanence in the world is asserted as well" (*SQC*, #II.B.5).

Unfortunately, the Council of Chalcedon did not resolve the many social and political problems between the differing factions. As a result, several large groups of Christians broke off and formed their own churches. The division between the Catholic Christians and the so-called Monophysite (one-nature) churches has lasted to the present day.[2] But for Catholic Christians, another foundation stone of Christology had been laid. Jesus Christ was (and is) confessed to be fully human as well as fully divine. And his humanity is not erased by the fact that the Word of God assumed it. Henceforward, the Catholic Christian tradition will speak of the divine and the human natures of Jesus Christ.

Later Christian thinkers and ecumenical councils developed the positions stated by the councils of Nicaea and Chalcedon even further. One of these key developments specified that the union of the two natures occurs precisely in the "person" (*hypostasis* in Greek) of the Son of God, the Second Person of the Trinity. (It is important to remember that "person" here does not mean our modern sense of a "center of psychological awareness" in the individual, but rather it intends an "underlying act of existence.") The underlying reality of Jesus Christ resides not in the human nature but in the divine nature. The Son of God, the Second Person of the Triune God, took on human nature and became an individual human being like us. This understanding became known as the "Hypostatic Union" and a part of Catholic Christian understanding to the present.

A second major development delineated just how profound and extensive was Jesus' assumption of our human nature. It was an acceptance of our total humanity, excepting sin. The Third Council of Constantinople in 681 would state: "We likewise proclaim in Him . . . two natural volitions or wills and two natural actions" (*CF*, p. 184). In his earthly life, Jesus thought, desired, willed, and acted as a human being, like all of us. This was the basis for the beautiful statement of the Second Vatican Council: "He worked with human hands, he thought with a human mind. He acted with a human will, and with a human heart he loved" (*GS*, #22). This full humanity of Jesus Christ needs to be especially recalled in our twenty-first century discussions and views of Jesus Christ.

# Two Approaches to Christology

These many disputes over Jesus Christ's identity, and the decisions of the ecumenical councils, would gradually result in a massive shift of emphasis within Catholic Christology. Through the centuries, and for many diverse reasons, more and more stress would be placed on the divinity of Jesus. He is really the Son of God come to earth. Therefore, every word spoken by Jesus in the Gospels can be considered a direct word of God. Although people formally acknowledged his full humanity as indicated in the creed, the practical import of that belief was seldom evident. This new approach differed from that of the first Christian centuries, which usually began with the mystery of the Resurrection of Jesus by God the Father. After the christological councils, the teaching of Christian communities shifted to highlight the centrality of the Incarnation, the act of the Son of God assuming human nature in the womb of the Virgin Mary. In this great divine action par excellence, the moment of salvation gradually took precedence over all else. This style of Christology may aptly be called an "incarnational theology."

The subsequent development of incarnational theology over many centuries ultimately contributed to the articulation of other beliefs in the Catholic Christian tradition. The Marian doctrines in particular (perpetual virginity, Immaculate Conception, Assumption into heaven) flow logically and naturally from this incarnational perspective. The divine privileges bestowed on Mary for her willing participation in such an amazing action were seen as an extension of salvific grace itself. Incarnational theology also led to a primary imaging of Jesus as the God-Man; the faithful believer must see "God" behind everything Jesus says or does, from his conception to his death and resurrection.

But problems also followed from this style of theology. Although the full humanity of Jesus may have been formally confessed, many Christians ceased thinking of Jesus as a human being who led a real religious life in first-century Palestine, struggling faithfully to live out his commitment, going to his death, and then being raised to a glorified life by a gracious and merciful God. Twentieth-century Catholic theologians in particular worried about other "gaps" that had developed in the whole schema of incarnational theology. The Resurrection of Jesus was often downplayed as a central and defining moment in the drama of salvation and instead, became simply another action that "proved" his divinity. Since the real struggles of life and faith in Jesus' career were not given full weight in preaching and catechesis, Christians lost the force of these mysteries as a guide for their own lives of faith.

In our time, many Catholic theologians have labored to reemphasize the importance of the Resurrection and Jesus' life history as starting points for Christology. In his book *Christology: A Biblical, Historical and Systematic Study of Jesus*, Gerald O'Collins explains a typical approach: "[H]istorical and liturgical considerations have persuaded me to make the resurrection of the crucified Jesus (with the outpouring of the Holy Spirit) the central focus. Historically, it was faith in and the proclamation of the paschal mystery that set the Christian movement going" (pp. 15–16). This approach begins with the life and ministry of Jesus, proceeds to the Resurrection, and then moves to the identity of Jesus Christ and the salvific effect of his work. It is sometimes called an "ascending" Christology, in contrast to a "descending" Christology, which starts with the Second Person of the Trinity and works "down" through the Incarnation, the life and ministry of Jesus, the Resurrection, and so on.

All Catholic believers should realize that both of these approaches have a legitimate standing in Catholic theology. The crucial point must be to affirm that, whichever approach one takes, the main aspects of the other approach are integrated and not forgotten and denied.

# Summary

Soon after the New Testament period, significant differences emerged between diverse Christian communities. This problem led to the formation of a Catholic Church tradition, whose major decision makers were the bishops meeting in council. The two ecumenical councils of Nicaea and Chalcedon formulated a basic doctrine or understanding of the identity of Jesus Christ, which has lasted to this day. The doctrine of two natures in the one person of Jesus Christ allows for the development of practical Christologies that may be either "ascending" or "descending."

## ENDNOTES

1. The italicized passages are those that the council wished to specifically stress.

2. For further information on these churches, see Robert Taft, ed. *The Oriental Churches in the United States* (Washington, DC: United States Catholic Conference, 1986).

# For Reflection

1. Are there current views of Jesus Christ that might be close to that of the Marcionites, Jewish Christians, and gnostics of old?

2. What would be some ways of explaining the technical words "nature" and "person" in more understandable, modern language?

3. Would you prefer to use an "ascending" or "descending" Christology in your catechesis? Give reasons for your choice.

# CHAPTER 4

# Further Christological Beliefs

ΙΧΘΥΣ

I n the early years after Jesus' death and Resurrection, his followers already had come to believe that more was involved in the Christ-event than the raising and vindication of Jesus, more even than a transforming event upon themselves through faith in him. They came to believe that in some way the basic relationship between God and all of creation had been affected for the better. They employed a wide variety of terms to express this fundamental change: redemption, salvation, expiation, justification, and reconciliation.

# Redemption and Salvation Through Jesus Christ

Saint Paul expressed this fundamental change in his Second Letter to the Corinthians. "[I]n Christ, God was reconciling the world to himself, not counting their trespasses against them. . . ." (5:19). The Acts of the Apostles confessed, "There is salvation in no one else, for there is no other name under heaven given among mortals by which we must be saved" (4:12). The Letter to the Hebrews put the same idea in a slightly different way: "For this reason he is the mediator of a new covenant, so that those who are called may receive the promised eternal inheritance" (9:15). In these and many more passages of the New Testament, we see that the early Christian faith believed that the whole Christ-event signaled a new and definitive bond between God and all creation.

Each of the biblical and theological terms used to express the basic relationship between God and all of creation—redemption, salvation, expiation, justification, reconciliation—possesses its own nuance of meaning. "Redemption" implies a type of "buying back" or "freeing from bondage." "Salvation" moves toward a condition of health or making whole. "Justification" places one in a state of uprightness before God. "Reconciliation" reunites that which had been separated. The common base remains that in Jesus Christ the basic relation between the mystery of God and all that exists was definitively changed for the better.

However phrased, this belief remained firmly among the fundamental faith convictions of the early Christian Church. It eventually came to be stated with great power and simplicity in the Creed of the Council of Nicaea: "For us men and for our salvation He came down, and became flesh" (*CF*, p. 6). The early Christian community and the great age of the Church councils were in basic agreement on this belief. The continuing discussions during the age of the first ecumenical councils (325–451) about how to express Jesus' nature and the relation of the divine and the human in him always returned to a fundamental principle that guided all doctrinal decisions: "what is not assumed is not saved." This meant that whatever the Second Person of the Trinity did not assume as the humanity of Christ had no chance of being saved. All was saved through Christ.

The Church continued to bear witness to the fundamental salvation effected by and in Jesus Christ. "He who did not withhold his own Son, but gave him up for all of us . . ." (Romans 8:32); "For God so loved the world that he gave his only Son, so that everyone who believes in him may not perish but may have eternal life" (John 3:16). On this topic the International Theological Commission comments, "If so, the person of Jesus Christ cannot be separated from the deed of redemption. The benefits of salvation are inseparable from the divinity of Jesus Christ" (*SQC*, #IV.A.1).

As the centuries continued, Christian thinkers tried to articulate more clearly how this basic change occurred. How, precisely, did Christ accomplish this "new change?" Was it through his death, his resurrection, or perhaps the Incarnation itself? What determined the time frame for this change? Was salvation definitively done, or perhaps only begun and now awaits a future completion? How do we see the effects of salvation in ourselves? Is it in the simple gift of faith, or a new knowledge, or a hope that looks to future fulfillment? Although many theologies of salvation and redemption waxed and waned in the Church's history, the Church never really decided many of these issues about salvation with the same precision as it did with regard to the identity of Jesus Christ. This point must be kept in mind with regard to the following section.

In the period of the church fathers (ca. 200–600), many theologians and others thought the fundamental change occurred through a redemptive incarnation. They used a strong descending Christology to see Jesus' becoming human as the way that led all humanity and creation to participate in the very reality of God. They were bold to speak of humanity's "becoming divine" (deification) through God's gift of grace. Saint Athanasius would boldly proclaim, "For he (the Word) became man that we might become divine" ("On the Incarnation," #54).

Other Christian thinkers took a more pessimistic view. They saw Christ's death as a ransom, a literal "buying back" of humanity from the devil, in whose grip it lay after the original sin. Unfortunately, this latter view could easily lead to an image of God as a "cruel father" sending his son to death to pay the "devil's ransom." During the medieval period in Western Europe (ca. 800–1400), Saint Anselm of Canterbury developed a famous redemption theology of satisfaction. In Anselm's view, God's honor had been marred by human sin and divine justice demanded that this honor be restored. This could be accomplished only by one who possessed equality with God and also shared fully as one of the human race. Therefore, the Son became incarnate—became fully human—to satisfy the past wrong, to identify with humanity, and to show—in the same action—the innate mercy of God.

During the late medieval period (1300–1500), a time of great social and religious confusion, many people slipped into almost magical views of salvation, believing, for example, that people could buy or ensure their salvation through the purchase of indulgences or the performance of popular religious practices. Such confused notions, and others like them, became an avalanche of factors that contributed to the Protestant Reformation (1517–1563). One of the cornerstones of the Reformation would be Martin Luther's theology of "justification." He emphasized that humanity was made upright or justified before God solely by God's free bestowal of faith and grace alone and not by any human effort. Luther's strong emphasis upon God's activity harkened back to Saint Paul's Letter to the Romans, especially chapters one to eight. Luther's theology challenged the Catholic Church to restate and sharpen its own belief in how God has saved us.

In response to the theology of the reformers as well as the widespread confusion among the Catholic faithful, the Ecumenical Council of Trent (1545–1563) formulated a statement about justification for the Roman Catholic Christian tradition. The council provided a clearer specification of the Catholic belief in salvation through Jesus Christ. It affirmed that "the Father in heaven . . . sent Jesus Christ his Son . . . that all might receive adoption as sons. Him God put forward as an expiation by his blood for our sins . . . but also for the sins of the whole world" ("Decree on Justification," p. 671). And to show that all justification (salvation) centers in Christ, it further decreed that "his most beloved and only begotten Son, our Lord Jesus Christ, . . . merited justification for us by his most holy passion on the wood of the cross, and made satisfaction to God the Father on our behalf" ("Decree on Justification," p. 673). The Catholic tradition once again grasped and clearly restated the New Testament belief that salvation is ultimately and totally God's gift in Jesus Christ.

Although originally formulated in different languages and styles of thinking, Catholic and Lutheran beliefs do not diverge by much. Roman Catholic and Lutheran Church leaders recently confirmed this recognition in the Joint Declaration on the Doctrine of Justification.

> 14. The Lutheran churches and the Roman Catholic Church have together listened to the good news proclaimed in Holy Scripture. This common listening, together with the theological conversations of recent years, has led to a shared understanding of justification.

15. In faith we together hold the conviction that justification is the work of the Triune God. The Father sent his Son into the world to save sinners. The foundation and presupposition of justification is the incarnation, death, and resurrection of Christ.

16. All people are called by God to salvation in Christ. Through Christ alone are we justified, when we receive this salvation in faith.

(as quoted in Origins 28 [July 1998]: 122)

In conjunction with the Church's belief in salvation and redemption through Christ, a related point of faith about Jesus Christ remains the subject of ongoing clarification: the centrality of the death of Jesus in the act of our salvation. Beyond God the Father sending the divine Son, Jesus—in his humanity, in his life history—freely gave himself for all humanity. His real willingness to give up his own life for the sake of others blossomed into the greatest gift his human love could bestow on humanity. "No one has greater love than this, to lay down one's life for one's friends" (John 15:13). The *CCC* stresses this point. "The desire to embrace his Father's plan of redeeming love inspired Jesus' whole life,[1] for his redemptive passion was the very reason for his Incarnation" (#607). In addition, that deliberate willingness to die "for us and our salvation" stands as the key revelation of God's love for us.

In more recent times, new theologies of salvation have emerged in Catholic Christian circles. Most of them seem concerned with developing an understanding of salvation through the perspective of an ascending Christology that begins with the human life and ministry of Jesus as their starting point. The practical example of Jesus thus provides the concrete model of how his followers become a part of the saving process. These theologies emphasize not so much a belief in redemption and salvation that is past but rather a salvation that begins in and struggles through the present age to find a glorious fulfillment in the future.

One such view of a present and future understanding of salvation emerged out of South American liberation theology. From a small beginning in the late 1960s, forms of liberation theology have appeared in many variations around the world. This theology stresses an image of Jesus as "the Liberator" of all people, but especially of the poor and oppressed. To liberation theologians, Jesus' teaching on the kingdom of God intended to help people build an honorable and just human society that recognizes all people as God's children. Jesus worked for the needy and the outcast as God's agenda. That commitment took him to his death, but the power of God raised him to a glorious life and vindicated his work of liberation. To enter God's salvation means to become part of Jesus' liberating work and vision for all the needy of the earth.

Salvation from a perspective of liberation requires the followers of Jesus to do the same things that he did. The faithful follower will actively involve him or herself with the social concerns and structures of society, especially when that society fails the weak, the poor, and the oppressed. In so doing, the believer enters the process of salvation begun by Jesus and awaits the fullness of that liberation in the Resurrection. The Resurrection stands as the ultimate hope of overcoming the earthly powers of evil. As liberation theologian Leonardo Boff says in his book titled Jesus the Liberator: "Jesus affected human beings at their very roots, activating their hope-principle and making them dream of the kingdom, which is not an entirely different world but this world completely new and renewed" (p. 79).

This new vision of Jesus and salvation received some confirmation from Pope Paul VI, although not with the same political urgency that liberation theologians espouse:

> As the kernel and center of his Good News, Christ proclaims salvation, this great gift of God which is liberation from everything that oppresses man but which is above all liberation from sin and the Evil One, in the joy of knowing God and being known by him, of seeing him, and of being given over to him. All of this is begun during the life of Christ and definitively accomplished by his death and Resurrection. But it must be patiently carried on

during the course of history, in order to be realized fully on the day of the final coming of Christ, whose date is known to no one except the Father.

(*On Evangelization in the Modern World*, #9, 10)

Most official Church documents have not been concerned with the "image of Jesus" in liberation theology; they care more about questions of the Church's involvement in society (social doctrine), which the liberation theology agenda aggressively promotes. One comment has been given, but it simply warns against tendencies to see Jesus just in political terms.[2]

Another version of a present-future theology of salvation asserts that Jesus did not simply "die" for our salvation, but that his whole life taught us a new meaning of being "human." We are saved precisely by entering fully and completely into the humanity of Jesus. The significance of this perspective is that Jesus does more than share our humanity; he also reshapes it through the example of his own life.

Those who believe in Jesus Christ must rethink what it means to be a human being in light of the life history of Jesus known from the Gospels. What we ordinarily assume to define as "humanity" from our cultural heritage or our contemporary intellectual learning does not suffice. The example of Jesus' life shows that human beings are created to seek God in love, in ser-vice, and in commitments to one another and, in so doing, work out their salvation (see Philippians 2:12–13). The mysteries of Christ's historical life, referred to in chapter 2, become pivotal moments in our vision of how to appropriate the salvation Jesus won for us. To follow this vision will ultimately lead to the cross of suffering fidelity. Because of God's graciousness and promise, Christians believe and look forward to the kingdom of God, to the full realization of salvation by and in this holy mystery.

This perspective of Catholic Christian belief was clearly enunciated to all the Church and the world in *GS*:

He who is the "image of the invisible God" (Colossians 1:15), is himself the perfect man who has restored in the children of Adam that likeness to

God which had been disfigured ever since the first sin. . . . If we follow [his] path, life and death are made holy and acquire a new meaning. (#22)

In a similar way the International Theological Commission encouraged the deepening of this perspective.

Jesus Christ is the perfect human being. . . . He is . . . the sacrament of the new humanity. The life of Christ affords us a fresh understanding of God and of man as well. Just as "the God of Christians" is new and specific, so too "the man of Christians" is new and original.

(*SQC*, #III.C.5)

Moreover, the commission acknowledged that this new way of thinking about the work of Christ and our salvation in Christ can take some getting used to.

A conception of human life derived from the life of Christ comes at first as a shock. This is indeed the reason why it demands conversion of everyone, and not only once at the beginning, but continuously, and, through perseverance, until the end. Such conversion as this can emerge only from a freedom renewed by love.

(*SQC*, #III.C.5)

This new way of entry into the whole of Christology offers fruitful opportunities for growth in faith. Believers come to see Jesus Christ challenging them to examine their own self-understanding as human beings, asking them to truly follow him, and so to receive the salvation he offers.

# Christology and Theology

As the belief in who Jesus Christ was and what he had accomplished continued to develop and be more clearly articulated in the Church, one driving force in the whole process was the discipline of theology. Theology as a science, or an organized system of thought, begins when religious thinkers apply an integral method of intellectual exploration, such as a particular philosophical or sociological system, to the beliefs of the Christian tradition. The purpose of this disciplined manner of thinking is to more clearly define religious language, to see and explore the relations of various beliefs to each other, to clear up confusions and contradictions, and to draw out implicit meanings in those beliefs that may not be evident at first glance.

Believers of every age have done this. Saints Paul and John the Evangelist were applying theology when they attributed various identifying titles to Jesus. Saint Justin Martyr was theologizing when he tried to understand the universality of Jesus Christ through the framework of Platonic philosophy. All the participants in the great ecumenical councils, like Saint Athanasius at Nicaea, sought to clarify and accurately express their belief in Jesus Christ.

The history of systematic Christian theology began in earnest in the second and third centuries. Christians, especially those from a Greek background and philosophical culture, pondered how to organize their Christian beliefs in order of importance—a vital concern for a people who were culturally primed to hierarchical and systematic thinking. Perhaps the best representative of this effort was a Christian thinker from Alexandria named Origen (ca. 185–253). In his book *On First Principles*, he took the framework of traditional Greek Platonic philosophy as a model for organizing the Christian beliefs of his time.[3] Doing so supplied a method for Christians raised in a Greek culture to understand the whole of Christian belief as an integrated system, to grasp it more clearly for themselves, and to use it in explaining the Christian faith to others. Theology has continued since then as a vital part of Catholic Christian life, a basic tool in developing and honing further expression of the basic belief in Jesus Christ. Over the centuries a wide variety of Christologies developed within the Christian tradition, such as the ascending and descending Christologies described in the previous chapter.

Although theologies show considerable variation, some distinctive characteristics mark those called Catholic Christian. First of all, faith, as the response to revelation, is understood to be a complex reality that touches all aspects of life. Therefore, theology grapples and dialogues with the entire spectrum of human life: politics, art, culture, daily life, and music. Second, a Catholic Christian theology necessarily involves a meditation upon Scripture. The sacred books contain the beginnings of our faith and present the first examples of genuine Christian faith in action. Third, theology builds on the Church's life; the community of faith is essential in Catholicism. Revelation is known and carried through the living history of the Church. The active worship of the community of faith decisively shapes its beliefs. The ancient adage *Lex orandi lex credendi* (The law of worship is the law of believing) bears eloquent witness to this characteristic. Fourth, Catholic Christian theology values critical thinking. This basic appreciation of human life remains fundamental to Catholicism. Finally, theology should work toward a commitment to the service of God's people.

The modern religious scene offers a plethora of academic and popular views about Jesus. Some of these theologies follow the characteristics of Catholic Christian theology and others do not. Trying to sort out and evaluate the myriad theologies can be quite confusing and daunting, not only for the average believer, but at times even for the pastoral minister. The following section addresses these concerns.

# Some Modern Concerns

Many modern Christologies have continued to develop even to our own day, connecting the figure of Jesus Christ to all aspects of religion and society. Often, these new ideas challenge the traditional beliefs of Catholic Christianity. To provide some guidelines, the International Theological Commission, a consultative arm of the Vatican's Congregation for the Doctrine of the Faith, has issued several documents in the last quarter century dealing with particular aspects of these various Christologies. A summary of these guidelines follows.

1. It is important that a balance be kept in presenting the humanity and divinity of Jesus. Both dimensions need clear expression. In particular, the belief in the eternal person of the Son of God really assuming the humanity of Jesus should not be downplayed in favor of the human person of Jesus simply revealing God (see Congregation for the Doctrine of the Faith, "Christ, the Trinity and Theology Today").

2. The specific connection between the earthly Jesus and the glorified Christ should not be overlooked. The very structure of the New Testament, in particular the Gospels themselves, shows at one and the same time a historical Jesus who was raised and glorified by the Father (see *SQC*, #I.B.2).

3. The language of the early ecumenical councils of the Church referring to Jesus Christ, like "person" and "nature," needs to be retained. However, the meanings of these terms are often understood differently in modern language and thought, and that difference should be noted (see *SQC*, #III.B.4).

4. Some modern Christologies have not adequately presented the essential connection between Christology and God's will to salvation. Jesus' ministry was not simply "for this earth." His whole life and death were for the salvation of all people and specifically a salvation that extends beyond this present life (see *SQC*, #IV.B).

5. The effect of the Holy Spirit in the human life of Jesus forms an essential element of Christology often overlooked today. The Spirit of God guides Jesus throughout his life and lives with him in all major events of his ministry. Increased knowledge of this point provides a solid basis for a Christian morality that takes its inspiration from the real life of Jesus (see *SQC*, #V.A).

6. The presentation of Christology always needs to be set in the context of its relation to other basic Christian beliefs, especially

the knowledge and revelation of the Triune God and the basic understanding of what it means to be human. Christology leads directly to Trinitarian belief. "The economy of Jesus Christ reveals the triune God" (see *TCA*, #I.C.1).

This brief survey of modern guidelines in the presentation of Christology leads back to the importance of a holistic perspective.

# Summary

The belief that all humanity and creation have been saved and redeemed in Christ found many explications in the Church's history. The key statements of the Council of Trent have been brought into modern ecumenical dialogue. The rise of theology as a disciplined manner of thinking contributed greatly to developments in Christology. Twentieth-century theology continued to find new ways to express the salvation won in Christ.

## Endnotes

1. *CCC* 607: Cf. *Lk* 12:50; 22:15; *Mt* 16:21–23.

2. Congregation for the Doctrine of the Faith, *Instruction on Certain Aspects of the Theology of Liberation* (Washington, DC: United States Catholic Conference, 1984): 27–28.

3. G. W. Butterworth, trans., *On First Principles* (Magnolia, MA: Peter Smith, 1991).

# For Reflection

1. What are some cultural factors that might affect Christian theology today, particularly in an understanding of salvation?

2. Examine in today's language ways of expressing how the basic relationship between God and creation was changed by Jesus?

3. Which modern concerns in Christology are most likely to crop up in today's classroom?

CHAPTER 5

Images
of
Jesus
Christ
in
Catholic Spirituality

Thus far we have considered the Catholic Church's basic doctrines about Jesus Christ. "Doctrines" refer to the Church's fundamental beliefs or convictions that lay a foundation, or provide a framework, for a fuller and richer presentation of the mystery of God-become-incarnate. To know Christ Jesus involves much more than holding certain convictions, however; it means entering into a living relationship—the heart and core of spirituality and prayer—with the Lord who inspires his followers as "the way, and the truth, and the life" (John 14:6). People who deeply believe need and want more than intellectual convictions; they desire a living, visual, and concrete expression of a real person with whom they can sense and feel and nurture a loving relationship. Thus, any complete Christology must also consider the many "images of Jesus" throughout the centuries of the Catholic tradition, as well as look for a suitable image of Jesus for our own time.

## The Meaning of an Image

An "image" of Jesus Christ implies more than a statement of meaning about his identity or salvific achievements. In this broader sense an image functions like a complex symbol that fuses together intellectual understandings, emotional responses, relational styles, and so on. An image of this breadth generally includes some specific visual traits that concretize how Christ looks, fits within his surroundings, and relates to people. An image of Christ fleshes out the basic framework of christological belief and creates a more complete human figure. Thus, an "image of Christ" goes beyond doctrine by adding specific elements to shape a concrete image of Jesus.

Frequently, these additional elements arise out of the personal and emotional concerns of the believers. These images of Christ carry a sense of how people understand their basic relationship to him and his relationship to them. A particular image often emphasizes one or two particular tenets of Christological belief more than others—not omitting the others but dealing with them in a more cursory manner. An image of Christ will usually include material from the culture people are familiar with; this material helps "fill in" the picture and gives it real-life qualities. Because of their personal, relational quality, images of Christ tend to develop and stress some particular form of prayer, some way of regularly relating with him who is the object of worship and devotion.

As an example to consider is the Sacred Heart, which functions beautifully as a modern "image of Christ." The Sacred Heart represents Jesus Christ as both divine and human and is an image that affirms the basic christological belief of the Catholic Church. But the image's particular focus highlights the infinite love of God shown through the human love of Christ. This love is visualized in pictures, statues, and holy cards of the Sacred Heart, usually depicted as a loving, sympathetic Jesus with a visible heart showing on his chest. The heart frequently "burns" with divine love, shooting rays of fire out to those around Jesus. Emotions elicited in the believer include a reciprocal love for God and for Christ demonstrated by prayer and acts of reparation for the many sins and outrages in the world. This love strives to continue loving even in the face of ingratitude. In the devotional and prayer traditions of the Sacred Heart, believers are called to frequent reception of Communion, especially on first Fridays of each month. Devotional writers have composed many written prayers and acts of consecration to the Sacred Heart formulated in a highly emotional style. The following provides one example:

> I give myself and consecrate to the Sacred Heart of our Lord Jesus Christ, my person and my life, my actions, pains and sufferings, so that I may be unwilling to make use of any part of my being save to honor, love and glorify the Sacred Heart. This is my unchanging purpose, namely, to be all His, and to do all things for the love of Him . . . renouncing with all my heart whatever is displeasing to Him. I therefore

take Thee, O Sacred Heart, to be the only object of my love, the guardian of my life, my assurance of salvation, the remedy of my weakness and inconstancy, the atonement for all the faults of my life and my sure refuge at the hour of death. Be then, O Heart of goodness, my justification before God Thy Father, and turn away from me the strokes of His righteous anger. O heart of love, I put all my confidence in Thee, for . . . I hope for all things from Thy goodness and bounty . . . let Thy pure love imprint Thee so deeply upon my heart, that I shall nevermore be able to forget Thee or to be separated from Thee; may I obtain from all Thy loving kindness the grace of having my name written in Thee, for in Thee I desire to place all my happiness and all my glory, living and dying in very bondage to Thee.

(Christopher, *The Raccolta*, p. 180)

The Sacred Heart image of Christ has been widespread in Catholic Church circles for many years. It surely specifies the basic christological doctrine of the Church, but its cultural background incorporates some additional themes. The image's strong emphasis on reparation originated in the tremendous emphasis on the Sacred Heart devotion during the Wars of Religion in Europe (ca. 1560–1650) and spread through the revelations of Saint Margaret Mary Alacoque. The religious responses called to this image of Christ call for mainly prayer and personal acts of reparation. The image as a whole places little emphasis on mission, service, or evangelization and can become quite privatized. Large aspects of Jesus' life and teaching are not given consideration in this particular image. When evaluating images of Christ, it is as important to focus on what is not emphasized as well as what is. The discussion will return to this point later.

At this point in examining images of Jesus Christ, we slide into the realm of spirituality, an area beyond both creed and theology that is generally not treated in technical Christologies. This separation, however, cuts off Christology from the flesh-and-blood religion of people. Let us take a moment to distinguish and relate doctrine and spirituality as elements of the complete faith expression of Catholic Christianity.

Doctrine, as mentioned above, refers to basic beliefs and convictions of faith; doctrine formulates what faith asserts to be believed. The creeds, which typify an end product of formulating doctrines, are collections of beliefs that have been accepted definitively by the Church as the clearest expression of its faith.

Spirituality, on the other hand, deals with the practical living out of that faith in the concrete settings of daily life. Spirituality touches where and how the universal faith ties into a particular time and place. It eludes exact description, but spirituality generally includes the following: (1) a deliberate and conscious striving by people (2) to integrate their faith convictions into the complex fabric of their real lives through a variety of prayers, devotional practices, artistic expressions, and practical activities (3) in order to enrich their lives and more deeply practice their faith. In more religious terminology, spirituality seeks a felt closeness to God and a real experience of the divine that deeply touches the human individual. The various images of Jesus Christ throughout history provide prime examples of spirituality in action.[1] Spirituality engages our total personality and historical uniqueness, the events and the history we live by, and our life settings. Spirituality usually absorbs cultural expressions from the society we live in. People borrow what they know, are comfortable with, and take for granted. Spirituality blends emotions, attitudes, and ideas into complex images and symbols.

The concrete forms in which a spirituality expresses itself (prayer, devotional practices, specific religious activities, and so on) differ greatly according to the circumstances of cultures, individuals' lives, and those particular aspects of faith such individuals deem to be most central and moving. Thus, spirituality can differ significantly by age group, gender, ethnic background, or marital status. The true "core" of spirituality is always hard to identify because it resides in that interior merging that takes place deep in the human heart.

Let us now proceed to examine several preeminent images of Jesus in Catholic Christian history.

# Images of Jesus

One of the first influential images of Jesus Christ appeared as the Incarnate Word of God. It became a most pervasive image during the patristic era of the Church (ca. 200–500). This image was also powerfully shaped by the influences of Greco-Roman culture. The tremendous power of Greek philosophy lay in its high estimation of the power of reason (thinking) and the importance of universality. For people of this heady culture, the image of Jesus Christ had to embody these values. Gradually, Christians themselves began to imagine Jesus in this same light. They came to highly revere the image of Jesus Christ as the Incarnate Word (Logos) of God—that is, the Logos that dwells in all things, in all people, as a power of rationality and a principle of order. Saint Athanasius, one of the great bishop-teachers of the early Church, put it this way:

> Seeing then all created nature, as far as its own laws were concerned, to be fleeting and subject to dissolution, lest it should come to this and lest the Universe should be broken up again into nothingness, for this cause He [God the Father] made all things by His own eternal word, and gave substantive existence to Creation, and moreover did not leave it to be tossed in a tempest in the course of its own nature, lest it should run the risk of once more dropping out of existence; but, because He is good He guides and settles the whole Creation by His own Word, Who is Himself also God, that by the governance and providence and ordering action of the Word, Creation may have light and be enabled to abide always securely.
>
> ("Against the Heathen," #41)

This image placed emphasis on Jesus as the Son of God—thus on the divine nature of Christ. The humanity of Jesus receives slight emphasis, for his humanness reminded these people of the limitedness and temporal aspects of Jesus. The real stress fell on Christ as salvation for the whole world. The humanity of Christ remained necessary to come to know the Logos, but the humanity of Jesus did not receive equal billing.

Connected with this image was a prayer style quite different from that known and practiced by most people today. Such a prayer looked much like an intellectual meditation and involved serious concentration and heavy thinking; the Greco-Roman world treasured the philosophical values of reason, order, and systematizing. Saint Augustine provides a good example of this type of prayer.

> In reading the Platonic books I found expressed in different words, and in a variety of ways, that the Son, "being in the form of the Father did not think it theft to be equal with God," because by nature he is that very thing. But that "he took on himself the form of a servant and emptied himself, was made in the likeness of men and found to behave as a man, and humbled himself being made obedient to death, even the death of the Cross so that God exalted him" from the dead "and gave him a name which is above every name, that at the name of Jesus every knee should bow, of celestial, terrestrial, and infernal beings, and every tongue should confess that Jesus is Lord in the glory of God the Father" (Philippians 2:6–11)—that these books do not have.
>
> (*Confessions*, pp. 121–122)

This image of Jesus Christ as the Incarnate Word of God remained prominent for many centuries. Although not the only image that flourished in the patristic era, this one did nourish many of the great teachers and Church writers of that time. The fruits of such meditations powerfully influenced the development of the Christological doctrines considered in chapter 3.

Centuries later a much different image of Jesus Christ, the Divine Bridegroom of the Soul, became the focal point of the spirituality of many believers. This image became prevalent in the eleventh and twelfth centuries after a new cultural sensitivity had taken shape in northern Europe. The world of classical antiquity had disappeared; the Germanic invasions and the subsequent conversions of those peoples were followed by centuries of political and social instability. Eventually, a new cultural synthesis arose—the flowering of medieval Europe—and by the year 1050, many people were seeking a new harmony and a renewed warmth in humanity. This cultural setting looked to an image of Christ that was warm and passionate to the individual believer, like an ardent spouse.

The Divine Bridegroom image of Christ carries strong, affective qualities. Jesus is named as a divine lover and friend. In this tradition occur some of the first and finest expressions of the tender motherliness of Jesus (Saints Anselm, Bernard, Aelred, Hildegard, Gertrude). The image of the Divine Bridegroom invites a highly emotional response from the believer. It affirms both the humanity and divinity of Jesus but seeks a stronger expression of Jesus as a divine lover who seeks the love of human hearts. This image carries little about the human psychology of Jesus, his particular life history, or his Jewish background.

The image of the Divine Bridegroom begets a unique style of prayer. This prayer becomes dialogic, person to person, like letters or intimate reflections to a friend. One of Saint Anselm's prayers demonstrates the graphic intimacy of this approach.

> Kindest, gentlest, most serene Lord,
> will you not make it up to me for not seeing
> the blessed incorruption of your flesh,
> for not having kissed the place of the wounds
>    where the nails pierced,
> for not having sprinkled with tears of joy
> the scars that prove the truth of your body?
> Alas, Lord, alas, my soul.
>
> (Ward, *The Prayers and Meditations*
> *of Saint Anselm*, pp. 153, 155)

The image of Christ as Divine Bridegroom of the Soul was also favored by many of the female mystics of medieval Europe and inspired them to prayers of the utmost personal devotion. Gertrude of Helfta addresses Christ in prayer:

> You are the overflowing abyss of divinity,
> Oh king of all kings most worthy,
> Supreme emperor,
> Illustrious prince,
> Ruler of infinite sweetness,
> Faithful protector,
> You are the vivifying gem of humanity's nobility,
> Craftsman of great skill,
> Teacher of infinite patience,
> Counselor of great wisdom,
> Most kind guardian,
> Most faithful friend,
> You are the delicate taste of intimate sweetness,
> Oh most delicate caresser,
> Gentlest passion,
> Most ardent lover,
> Sweetest spouse,
> Most pure pursuer.
> (as quoted in Bynum, *Jesus as Mother: Studies in the Spirituality of the High Middle Ages*, pp. 187–188)

This image of Christ recognized his divinity but saw it revealed in a humanity that fervently sought a loving relationship with each soul. The nurturing of that bond in an expressive love became the hallmark of a mystical spirituality that nourished the lives of many medieval saints.

Jumping forward two hundred years, we encounter a third image of Jesus Christ quite different from the previous two: the Suffering Crucified Savior. The social world of medieval unity had collapsed by the early fourteenth century; there was no longer any trusted foundation in society, and anxiety ran rampant through people's lives. The fourteenth century had to endure major traumatic events—the self-imposed papal exile in Avignon; the black plague that wiped out a third of the population of Western Europe; the Hundred Years War between England and France— all of which proved the insecurity of human institutions, the brutality of life, and the painful reality of imminent death. This age knew great physical suffering, excruciating deaths, and much psychological despair. To deal with these traumas, the image of Jesus as a suffering, crucified savior appeared. He was still both God and man, but the emphasis fell clearly on a savior who could identify with human pain and still save us.

This image of Jesus appeared visually as a broken, torn, bleeding man on a cross. It showed vividly Jesus' mangled, blood-covered skin and depicted him as aware that he was close to death. To the people of that era, Jesus suffered their physical pain and anguish; he knew so well their constant closeness to death. The portrayal of his suffering and agony became vivid and realistic, even grotesque at times. Spiritual writers concentrated on the biblical accounts of Christ's passion (being stripped, mocked, beaten, and nailed) and applied these indignities to human life. Devotions to the cross, the holy face, and the wounds and blood escalated within this spirituality.

The style of prayer associated with the Suffering Crucified Savior had at one time a quality of heartfelt pleading, at another a simple gazing at the pain of Jesus with the knowledge that he feels ours, too. This bond did not exude the warm closeness of the Divine Bridegroom or the intellectual stimulation of the Incarnate Word. Meditations on the wounds of Christ and his death, such as litanies, the Way of the Cross, and the Dies Irae were composed by many believers, and all of these meditations reflected the image of Jesus as our crucified, suffering Savior. Perhaps the flavor of this prayer is best captured through the words of the "Stabat Mater," a great hymn of the early fourteenth century:

> At the cross her station keeping,
> Stood the mournful Mother weeping,
> Close to Jesus to the last.
> Through her heart, His sorrow sharing,
> All His bitter anguish bearing,

Lo! the piercing sword had passed.
O how sad and sore distressed
Was that Mother, highly blessed,
Of the sole-begotten One.
Woe-begone, with heart's prostration;
Mother meek, the bitter Passion
Saw she of her glorious Son.
Who on Christ's dear Mother gazing,
In her trouble so amazing,
Born of woman, would not weep?
Who on Christ's dear Mother thinking,
Such a cup of sorrow drinking,
Would not share her sorrow deep?
For His people's sins rejected,
Saw her Jesus unprotected,
Saw with thorns, with scourges rent:
Saw her Son from judgment taken,
Her Beloved in death forsaken,
Till His spirit forth He sent.

(*The Raccolta*, pp. 270–271)

At a time when people needed an image of Christ they could "relate to" with their pain and despair, the Suffering Crucified Savior spoke the whole Gospel to them. In many ways this image has never left the Church; people of every age, time, and country have returned to variations on this theme.

Consider one final image of Jesus Christ in Catholic spirituality: our Divine Savior. This image arose during the time of the Counter-Reformation, the Catholic reaction to the Protestant Reformation (ca. 1600–1700). Protestant Christians had attacked Roman Catholic policy and practice, asserting a radical difference between the simple image of Jesus in the New Testament and the rich and powerful institution the Catholic Church had become. In the minds of Protestant Christians, Catholics could not be called true Christians. The Catholic reaction, therefore, imaged a Jesus Christ who was the Divine Savior come to earth in human form with a divine plan: to set up a church, the Roman Catholic Church.

The key elements of this image of Christ revolved around the establishment of this Church: Jesus Christ appointed leaders (apostles, bishops) to be guides; he taught doctrines (Church dogmas) to live by; and he instituted sacraments (all seven) for spiritual strength.

The qualities of the Divine Savior strongly favored the divinity of Jesus Christ. To carry out his plan, the Savior was always calm, serene, in control, on top of every situation, knowing the thoughts of others—always carrying out his work of salvation with resolve. Everything looked forward to establishing the Catholic Church. This image did not dwell on the human psychology of Jesus, his dealing with his own vocation and ministry, or his life events as mysteries for us to imitate.

Prayers to the Divine Savior were, in particular, the official prayers to Christ as God, as the one who has saved us by establishing the Church and all it possesses. Christ was, above all, venerated in the Blessed Sacrament. Traditional prayers to Mary also tied in with this image, for prayers to Mary persuaded her to intercede with her divine Son.

We have considered four prominent images of Jesus Christ within the Catholic tradition. There could have been many more. Taken together they show how vividly the one body of faith gives rise to many practical expressions (because of the connection to the various concrete life settings of people). These four have all been strong and valid images of Christ in the Catholic tradition, and they all probably still resonate for some believers today. There's nothing wrong with that; each image can fit in with the lives of some believers today.

# Christology and Spirituality

An understanding of the images of Jesus Christ is important for evangelization and catechesis. Images of Jesus need connection with official Church teaching on Jesus Christ. One task of pastoral leadership is to effectively blend Catholic doctrine with the very real images of Jesus Christ that hold sway in people's lives right now. These images help people enter into a personal, living, and prayerful relationship with Christ. As Alyward Shorter says in *Toward a Theology of Inculturation*:

> The end result of evangelization—the proclamation of the Gospel of Jesus Christ—is to enable the one who is evangelized to recognize the presence of Jesus Christ in his or her own life, both individual and communal. . . .the one who is evangelized is enabled to have a transforming encounter with the crucified and risen Lord. (p. 61)

If ministers are to be effective they should also concern themselves with examining and evaluating people's Christ images. The images of Christ being shaped in people's lives usually contain powerful emotional material and cultural perceptions that meet the personal needs of the individual. Not every aspect of people's Christ image, however, may be historically true about Jesus or an accurate reflection of the Church's teaching on other religious issues. A serious task, therefore, is to help people—both children and adults—establish a dialogue between three perspectives: their image of Christ; the Church's doctrine about Christ; and what is known historically about Jesus. *Jesus Christ, Word of the Father* (the official catechetical text in preparation for the Holy Year of 2000), prepared by the Theological-Historical Commission for the Great Jubilee of the Year 2000, speaks to this issue.

> The mystery of Jesus Christ is a central element in popular piety. The popular Christ—at whatever level he is understood or "distorted" theologically—is a Christ who is lived, heard, welcomed, loved, and followed by the Christian people. However disfigured and poor may be the reasons for this devotion—often to the advantage of the Blessed Virgin and the saints—this Christ nonetheless illumines and sustains the existence of the people as a whole, becoming the bearer and the guarantor of its noblest

values and of its oldest aspirations. . . . This popular christology calls for a catechesis aimed at a reevangelization that announces without reduction or preconceptions the biblical-ecclesial figure of Christ, true God and true man. (pp. 44–45)

Several distinct steps in this dialogue might be noted. First, pastoral ministers should affirm the need for a strong image of Christ in people's lives. The beliefs of real people become specified and concretized most often through a devotional response to a specific image. In this way, the Gospel acquires a relevance and legitimacy in their lives. Pastoral ministers may need to exercise some leniency regarding the images of Christ they encounter in people's lives. Emotional values in images are altered only with great patience.

Second, the power of each image of Christ should be judged in relation to the Church's doctrinal teaching about Jesus Christ and scriptural investigations into the life of Jesus. Doing so may then invite further adjustment of the image. For example, it would be easy to have an over-politicized view of Jesus (as completely given to challenging the worldly powers of this earth); or, just as easily, people might have an apolitical view of Jesus. The task then will be to look carefully at what historical study reveals to us about the involvement of the historical Jesus with the social and political powers of his time. Critical history plays a decisive role here. The same would be true of an overly divine or overly human image of Jesus Christ. In all these cases catechists and pastoral ministers can help people see the need for amending a particular image.

Third, pastoral ministers should help people in relating their particular images of Jesus Christ to a concrete end in Christian service. Jesus came to serve and give his life for many; he gave to his disciples a very specific example and mandate to that effect at the Last Supper. People need to explore specifically how their image of Christ connects them to real mission and service and gives guidance and strength along the way.

Lastly, pastoral ministers should help people relate their images of Christ to their ways of praying so that these two aspects of a healthy Christian life may truly nourish each other.

## Summary

Images of Jesus Christ touch a broader area than Church doctrine. They are expressions that connect with people's emotions and personal concerns; they make Jesus understandable in terms of the culture people live in. Specific images also inspire particular forms of prayer. Images belong to the realm of spirituality, which must also be considered in the scope of a total Christology. The Incarnate Word of God, the Divine Bridegroom of the Soul, the Crucified Suffering Savior, and our Divine Savior all served as prominent images of Christ at various periods in the Church's history. One of the goals for all pastoral ministers is to blend the Church's fundamental doctrines about Jesus Christ into images that allow people to relate to him personally and to pray to him deeply.

### Endnote

1. An excellent book that provides thorough descriptions and analyses of images of Christ discussed above is Jaroslav Pelikan, *Jesus Through the Centuries: His Place in the History of Culture* (New Haven, CT: Yale University Press, 1985).

# FOR REFLECTION

1. Identify images of Christ present today in the Church, in homes, in popular media, in culture, and in your parish.

2. What kinds of meanings are embedded in these images of Christ? Do they give rise to prayer? Do they provide any kind of emotional connection or moral direction for Christian living?

3. How do these images of Christ correlate with basic Catholic doctrine about Jesus Christ?

# CHAPTER 6

# Christ with Us Today

One of the greatest Christological beliefs of the New Testament holds that the presence of Jesus Christ remains in the midst of his disciples. "'For where two or three are gathered in my name, I am there among them'" (Matthew 18:20). "'And remember, I am with you always, to the end of the age'" (Matthew 28:20). This conviction has endured throughout the Catholic Christian tradition. This closeness and nearness of Christ is believed and expressed in a number of ways.

# The Enduring Presence of Christ in the Church

The strongest assertion of this belief states that Christ is actually present in the eucharistic celebration. The consecrated bread and wine really become the Body and Blood of the Lord, and during the celebration his sacramental presence enters into believers in the deepest way possible. "The mode of Christ's presence under the Eucharistic species is unique. It raises the Eucharist above all the sacraments as 'the perfection of the spiritual life and the end to which all the sacraments tend.'"[1]

That presence, however, does not constitute the sole presence of Christ in the Church and the world. Jesus comes close to believers in many ways during the entire eucharistic action.

> Christ is always present in his Church, especially in her liturgical celebrations. He is present in the Sacrifice of the Mass not only in the person of his minister, . . . but especially in the eucharistic species. By his power he is present in the sacraments. . . . He is present in his word since it is he himself who speaks when the holy scriptures are read in the Church. Lastly, he is present when the Church prays and sings.
>
> (Sacrosanctum Concilium
> [The Constitution on the Sacred Liturgy], #7)

The council fathers called on the Catholic faithful to also recognize the presence of Christ in the priest-celebrant, in the readings from the Bible, in the whole praying congregation, and in the consecrated bread and wine. Indeed, these multiple presences should strengthen and accent one another.

This presence and closeness of Jesus in the ongoing lives of his disciples today elevate him above a memory or past event. He surely did live at a particular time and in a definite place, but his presence, the real core of his being, truly continues with his followers and believers. As the Third Children's Eucharistic prayer asserts so directly, "Jesus now lives with you in glory, but he is also here on earth, among us" (*Eucharistic Prayers for Masses with Children and for Masses of Reconciliation*, #28). We need to explore more fully this key aspect of Catholic Christology.

For all its common usage in both technical and popular religious language, the term *presence* does not easily yield precise definitions. In fact, when examined closely, *presence* provides a wide spectrum of meanings. Whenever we speak of the "presence of Christ" or the "presence of God," we must ask, What kind of presence? This crucial issue in catechesis about the mystery of Jesus Christ among us needs further exploration, and it will carry us into some technical thinking.

Usually, the first understanding of "presence" that comes to mind in the common language of most people today reflects a meaning strongly influenced by the psychological tenor of the times. Here the word stands for the direct awareness and attention "of two subjects to each other," a kind of eyeball-to-eyeball experience. It occurs when two people are personally aware of and interacting with each other—and are immediately and mutually aware of the bond between them. Let's call this kind a physical, conscious, personal presence. It carries great significance to many people because of the personal one-to-one implications and the consoling, supportive care that can easily accompany it. It is also the kind of presence that many believers wish to have with Jesus and God. This understanding of presence can exert a powerful force in a religious setting but can also cause problems if it functions as the only understanding of religious presence we know and seek. In that instance, people become confused and discouraged if it is absent.

The word *presence* can also mean the presence of things that I can sense not as personal subjects but as objects. The clock ticking on my desk is present to me; I can see, hear, and touch it. The clock possesses a simple physical presence to me. That particular presence does not enter much into religious discussion today.

Still another meaning of *presence* occurs when I bring up memories or form images of persons who were or are important in my life. I can imagine these persons and the effects they had or have on me right now; this type of psychological presence in my awareness can move me minimally or powerfully. Often, the image of Jesus that I shape in my mind when reading the Gospels functions as a psychological presence.

We should also recall that the general use of the word *presence* has not always referred to the psychological realm alone but stretches into the larger realms of knowledge and reality. For example, from science I believe in the underlying atomic structure of everything physical—a reality that remains "present" to me as a basic principle of life. Yet I do not relate to it personally; I do not sense it; and I can only dimly imagine it. It becomes a principled presence. It's there because of the way I look at reality as a whole; I acknowledge the fact, but it doesn't strike any resonant personal chords. On the other hand, a variant of this usage of *presence* may be that of a principle which I know and which *does* exert a sensed pressure upon me. Gravitation, for example, is an underlying principle that I sense very directly in certain circumstances of life, such as when I slip on ice. This is an active principled presence.

All of these different meanings need to be kept in mind and explained when we come to the use of the word *presence* in religious settings and, most surely, when speaking of the presence of Jesus Christ in the sacraments, in the Bible, and so on. Indeed, from the very beginning, the followers of Jesus—after the Resurrection—tried to express just how the presence of Christ was "with them." One explanation saw Jesus' presence "in the Spirit" as a creative power from within the individual or collective body. "Now the Lord is the Spirit" (2 Corinthians 3:17) carries an understanding of something like an active psychological presence that holds a powerful sway over us. Another way of describing Christ's presence was in terms more reflective of a "permanent principle" always at hand. "Do you not know that your bodies are members of Christ?" (1 Corinthians 6:15). This kind of presence in terms of bodiliness functioned like an active principled presence more than any others. It underlies our very reality.

The Gospel story of the two travelers on the way to Emmaus (see Luke 24:13–35) integrates several senses of Jesus' presence. Over the course of the narrative, the travelers come to recognize Jesus in the Scriptures, in the mysterious stranger, in their hearts, as well as in the breaking of the bread.

> When he was at the table with them, he took bread, blessed and broke it, and gave it to them. Then their eyes were opened, and they recognized him; and he vanished from their sight. They said to each other, "Were not our hearts burning within us while he was talking to us on the road, while he was opening the scriptures to us?"
>
> (24:30–32)

These same distinctions about presence emerge in comparing the various images of Christ explored in the last chapter. The spirituality that adored Jesus Christ as the Incarnate Word dealt with and prayed to him much like a type of active principled presence in the entire universe that welled up in their lives. Jesus is the Logos, the Word that infuses and upholds all things, including our very lives. But this Logos operates as a silent, pervasive principle of reality, a genuine presence that permeates everything.

A different sense of presence dominates the image of Christ as the Divine Bridegroom of the Soul. Here the presence of Jesus appears as a direct psychological presence, conscious and personal, whose emotions are communicated directly to our emotions. Such intense psychological presence exerts a persuading influence over us; we speak to this presence of Jesus as a specific imaged individual.

When the Council of Trent (1545–1563) affirmed a "real presence" of Jesus Christ in the Eucharist, it was affirming a type of presence more akin to an active principled presence, not one that was necessarily conscious and psychological. The *CCC* emphasizes this point.

> This presence is called "real"—by which is not intended to exclude the other types of presence as if they could not be "real" too, but because it is presence in the fullest sense: that is to say, it is a *substantial* presence by which Christ, God and man, makes himself wholly and entirely present.
>
> (#1374, emphasis in original; as quoted from
> *Mysterium Fidei [On the Holy Eucharist]*, #39)

The deepest reality and meaning of this "event" of the eucharistic bread and wine confesses the core reality of Jesus Christ as always present in the Eucharist, whether we consciously sense it or not. The grace of the sacrament comes to the believer even if the "conscious presence" of Christ may seem absent.

Of course, the fullest reception of the Eucharist brings the other meanings of *presence* into full play. In that instance the active power of an individual's faith will assist other meanings of presence to build upon the basic principled presence. It would not just be that underlying reality, believed in faith; it would also be a psychological presence that reminds us directly of the Jesus of Nazareth known in memory and imagination. That provides an imaged presence so vivid that it becomes a personal, conscious presence of Jesus Christ to us and the whole eucharistic community. Herein lies the fullest and richest sense of "communion" with Jesus Christ in the Eucharist.

> Communion with Jesus Christ, by its own dynamic, leads the disciple to unite himself with everything with which Jesus Christ himself was

profoundly united: with God his Father, who sent him into the world, and with the Holy Spirit, who impelled his mission; with the Church, his body, for which he gave himself up, with mankind and with his brothers whose lot he wished to share.

(*GDC*, #81)

Throughout history the presence of Jesus Christ to his followers has remained one of the building blocks of Catholic Christology. The understanding of Christ's presence in the Eucharist provides the model for a basic grasp of the general sacramental presence of Christ in Baptism, Confirmation, Matrimony, and so on. Every sacrament possesses the same principled presence of Christ in the Eucharist. That reality of Christ perdures in the sacrament simply because of God's promise, whether or not an individual consciously senses it or not. The living and active faith of believers, however, can bring that presence into a more immediate, personal, and transforming presence enlivened by the image of Jesus known from the Gospels. That should be the goal of good sacramental celebration, preaching, and effective catechesis. The sacrament of Baptism, for example, should be a true joining of our lives with the mystery of Jesus Christ and the mysteries of his own life. Similarly, the sacrament of Reconciliation should be an encounter with the presence of the merciful Jesus known as the one who forgives sinners. All of the sacraments should encourage a multiple experience of the presence of Christ.

# Christ's Presence in Prayer

One important presence of Jesus Christ that happens in the lives of many believers occurs in prayer. When Christians seek a direct and personal connection to God or Christ, many come to know a divine presence in ways that move them profoundly. Just as does Christ's presence in the sacrament, Christ's presence in prayer is a preeminent example of Christ's support and care in the lives of his disciples today.

Jesus becomes a true leader and guide in prayer by the example of his own life. The Christian tradition of prayer looks to the prayer of Jesus to find its clearest expression. The specific and unique prayer life of Jesus can provide the foundation for all Christian prayer, and it remains the starting point to which we must continually return. The Letter to the Hebrews confesses Jesus as "the pioneer and perfecter of our faith" (12:2), and nowhere is this more accurate than in Jesus' example of praying. "That Jesus prayed is one of the best documented aspects of the historical Jesus" (*Jesus Christ, Word of the Father*, p. 131). Although he surely had a profound teaching on prayer, knowing how he prayed can help us get in touch with his powerful psychological presence in our prayer, a very conscious personal presence that encourages, supports, and carries us along.

> It is useful to rediscover Christian prayer today by contemplating the icon of Jesus in prayer. This is a fascinating side of Jesus' personality that has created an authentic, millennial tradition of Christian spirituality and holiness that is waiting to be rediscovered and to be made the most of. Jesus' originality in this field has been grasped even by non-Christians, who see in him not only a pious Jew, but above all an unsurpassable master of spiritual life and intimacy with God.
>
> (*Jesus Christ, Word of the Father*, p. 131)

Two further preliminary points need to be made. First, the basic notion of prayer, as used by New Testament writers, possesses a wider horizon than many Christians may realize. Too often, people think of praying as the recitation of set formulas of traditionally composed prayers, like the Our Father or the Hail Mary, or of specific postures such as kneeling. These are truly valid forms of prayer, but the basic reality of what prayer encompasses extends further. The act of "praying" describes any basic conscious attention directed toward the reality of God and the relationship between God and ourselves. So, wherever and whenever we consciously attend to God and the quality of the bond between us, we are praying. There can be many kinds and qualities of direct attention—joyful, angry, apprehensive—and they can last a minute or an hour. They can take place in church, at the office, or in the car. What does matter is the focus of that attention; when directed toward God, it is prayer!

A second preliminary point calls us to remember that the human Jesus was born into and lived his whole life in a Jewish religious culture. His parents would have taught him the ancient ways of the People of Israel. Jesus prayed in the style of a first-century Jew and was the heir of a religious tradition richly steeped in ways of praying. Knowing this background of Jewish prayer can help us enormously. It expands the slight amount of material we know from the Gospels into a much richer panorama. As we explore the style and depth of Jesus' prayer, we may touch his imaged presence in a way that has a powerful effect upon our own prayer. As we pray with him, he prays with us. His presence strengthens us and becomes a way through which the real grace and strength of God enters powerfully into our lives and faith.

## IN DAILY LIFE AND WORK

It may come as a surprise to learn that the primary setting in which Jesus would have prayed was his daily routine of life and work. The prayer that most marked the pious Jew was (and is) the praying of the *Shema*, that fundamental expression of Jewish faith: "Hear, O Israel: The Lord is our God, the Lord alone. You shall love the Lord your God with all your heart, and with all your soul, and with all your might" (Deuteronomy 6:4–5). It was the responsibility of the observant Jew to pray at least three times a day— morning, late afternoon, and evening—wherever one was (home, marketplace, field) and whatever one was doing (working, relaxing, spending time with friends). The *Shema* called to mind and expressed the reality of Israel's God and the relationship between God and Israel, and between God and the individual believer.

After the *Shema*, a pious Jew added two other types of daily prayer. One was the *Berakot*, benedictions or blessings of God's greatness and doings. A *berakah* was essentially a praise of God's goodness in some area of human life. "Blessed are You, Lord our God, King of the Universe, who brings forth bread from the earth." The second type of daily prayer was called the *Tefillot*, prayers that beseeched God for one's own needs. "Bless this year for us, O Lord our God, and all its varied produce that it be good for; provide dew and rain as a blessing on the face of the earth."

After the recitation of the *Shema*, according to their circumstances of life, the believer will add several *Berakot* and *Tefillot*. These prayers were not long but, recited regularly, created a framework for the individual's day, three times a day, every day, that bound a believer to God. Such were the form of Jesus' daily prayers.

Another type of usual Jewish prayer, similar to the above but a bit more flexible in style, would have been the spontaneous expression of thanksgiving or praise to God that erupted in a given moment. Several times the Gospels show Jesus using this form of prayer.

> *I thank you, Father, Lord of heaven and earth,*
> *because you have hidden these things from the wise*
> *and the intelligent and have revealed them to infants.*
>
> (Matthew 11:25)

> *Father, I thank you for having heard me. I knew that*
> *you always hear me, but I have said this for the sake*
> *of the crowd standing here, so that they may*
> *believe that you sent me.*
>
> (John 11:41–42)

This type of prayer was not formal but was adapted to each situation and its circumstances. It recognized God's connection to everything that happened in people's lives.

When Jesus' disciples asked him to teach them how to pray, Jesus gave them a series of prayers in the form of just such short expressions: "'Our Father in heaven,/hallowed be your name./Your kingdom come./Your will be done. . . .'" (Matthew 6:9–10). The Magnificat of Mary carries the same basic structure of short spontaneous prayer: "'My soul magnifies the Lord, and my spirit rejoices in God my Savior. . . .'" (Luke 1:46–47). Christians should say these fine prayers just as they are, but as words of the Bible these prayers should also inspire occasions for people to begin their own unique expressions of praise, thanksgiving, and need that spring from the particular events of their lives. In praying this way, we find ourselves again praying the way of Jesus.

Christians who wish to join Jesus in prayer and to meet him in prayer daily should use the rhythm of the day as a key for remembering their basic connection to God; they should use it to be thankful, to praise, to ask, to be watchful, and to remember. Daily prayers form a framework for sanctifying the time of our lives, day in and day out, reminding us of God and our relationship to God. They also bring us into the presence of Christ by identifying with him and praying as he did. Very likely this regular, daily routine of mindful prayer was precisely what Saint Paul had in mind when he wrote to the Christians in Thessalonica: "Rejoice always, pray without ceasing, give thanks in all circumstances. . . ." (1 Thessalonians 5:16–18). Toward the end of the first century Christians would substitute the "Our Father" for the Shema as the prayer to be said three times a day.[2] This may still serve as a regular personal daily prayer for Christians, who will then add their own instances of praise and need.

## In Official Places of Worship

Jesus would have prayed regularly in the synagogue and at the Temple in Jerusalem, the official public places of prayer for the pious and faithful Jew. In these settings the prayers would have tended to be more traditional and fixed. For example, certain prayer rituals were said at the offering of sacrifices in the Temple. Many of the Psalms come from such prayer rituals. Some prayers were to be said on the way to Jerusalem and the Temple; others were prayers upon entering the Temple; still others were thanksgivings or pleas for help that accompanied the offering of Temple sacrifices by the priests. The moods and tempers of the Psalms are manifold; they speak to all aspects, emotions, and situations of human life.

Jesus would have prayed the Psalms regularly, and their individual passages would have been part of his regular address to

God, his Father. His words of anguish on the cross, "My God, my God, why have you forsaken me?" (Mark 15:34), for example, are the opening words of Psalm 22. Certain Psalms Jesus likely would have learned by heart, to be prayed on official occasions as well as when he was alone.

The followers of Jesus, themselves rooted in the same Jewish prayer tradition, cherished the Psalms. In fact, the church fathers often called the Psalms the prayer book of the early Christian Church. In praying them, we, too, pray as Jesus did. His lips prayed, just as ours do:

> I love you, O Lord, my strength.
> The Lord is my rock, my fortress, and my deliverer,
>     my God, my rock in whom I take refuge,
>     my shield, and the horn of my salvation, my
>         stronghold.
> I call upon the Lord, who is worthy to be praised,
>     so I shall be saved from my enemies.
> The cords of death encompassed me;
>     the torrents of perdition assailed me;
> the cords of Sheol entangled me;
>     the snares of death confronted me.
> In my distress I called upon the Lord;
>     to my God I cried for help.
> From his temple he heard my voice,
>     and my cry to him reached his ears.
>                                        (Psalm 18:1–6)

In praying the Psalms we learn not only a correspondence with the joys, hopes, sorrows, and losses of human life and their relation to God, but we can also grasp a deeper appreciation for the "official prayers" of Church liturgy and sacrament. In these prayers of the Mass and sacraments, we find composed and fixed prayers, like the eucharistic prayers and others that accompany actions of consecrating, blessing, anointing, and so on. Knowing the setting of the Psalms may help us appreciate these prayers as heartfelt expressions of our life with the mystery of God.

## IN THE PRIVACY OF OUR HEARTS

Noted often in the Gospels was Jesus praying alone.

> *[H]e went up the mountain by himself to pray.*
>
> (Matthew 14:23)

> *In the morning, while it was still very dark, he got up and went out to a deserted place, and there he prayed.*
>
> (Mark 1:35)

> *Now during those days he went out to the mountain to pray; and he spent the night in prayer to God.*
>
> (Luke 6:12)

The Gospels also depict Jesus praying before special moments and events in his life: at his Baptism (see Luke 3:21); before the Transfiguration (see Luke 9:28); before calling the disciples (see Luke 6:12); praying for Peter's faith (see Luke 22:31–32). In none of these moments do we know exactly how Jesus prayed, but the Gospels do offer an insight indicating that his personal prayer reflected the sense of an intimate and deeply personal contact with God. An intimation of this contact comes from his use of the familiar term *Abba* (Father) for God. Much has been written about the significance of Jesus' use of this term. For our purposes we might note simply that to address the mystery of God in such personal and familiar terms highlights the kindness of God as a loving father, a caring parent.

The very language of God as Abba-Father also accents the depth of intimacy into which one may enter into prayer with God. This type of inner prayer may be conversational, in which nothing is held back, akin to the conversation of deep friendship. On the other hand, this intimacy may simply find expression in a profound and peaceful silence, a great inner quietness that is itself a prayer. The intimacy of Jesus' prayer with his Abba becomes the originating point for the later development of contemplative prayer in the Christian tradition.

## In Temptation and Suffering

A final instance of Jesus' prayer happens in the Garden of Gethsemane (see Mark 14:32–36). Many Christians know this prayer all too well—a prayer joined to the fear of suffering and distress. In Luke's account the presence of bloody sweat shows the intense physical reaction of Jesus' body to the threat of pain; mental and spiritual suffering overflows into his body. In those moments the fullness of Jesus' human condition expressed itself clearly. Jesus did not want to suffer or experience pain, and that desire became a part of his prayer: "'Father, if you are willing, remove this cup from me; yet, not my will but yours be done'" (Luke 22:42).

The prayer of the Garden of Gethsemane continues into the Passion narrative. Everything in the Passion stories connects to pain of some kind: the humiliation before Pilate, the mocking of the soldiers, the betrayal of a trusted friend, the realized separation from loving family members, the scourging, the way of the cross, the nailing, the hours of agony while his body was being torn apart. In the last and perhaps most poignant moment of the Jesus Passion story is the cry of desperation, "My God, my God, why have you forsaken me?" (Mark 15:34). His body torn apart by human cruelty, frightened to the core of his being, Jesus knew he was about to die. He cried out in words that jumbled together despair (fear of an answerless void) with prayer (a basic trusting connection with God).

Jesus' prayers in Gethsemane and on the cross carry a single message for Christian spirituality, one that touches directly on the connection between prayer and suffering in the lives of all believers: it is all right to want to avoid suffering. It is all right to fear an upcoming suergery, to worry about the medical treatment, and to be anxious about a routine trip to the dentist. We might take this insight a step further and assert that the acceptance of suffering as part of our humanity and a way to salvation touches the deepest part of Christian spirituality. The burden of accepting our created humanity in suffering shows the very mystery of humanity to be almost as impenetrable as the mystery of God.

Prayer flows as the true lifeblood of a strong spiritual life, an attentiveness that prepares us to listen as well as openly communicate with the mystery of God. In addition, the practice of prayer according to the example of Jesus can be a special moment that brings us into a very real presence of Christ in our lives.

## Summary

Christians believe that the powerful, loving, and supportive presence of Jesus Christ remains in their lives always. He is present in the eucharistic bread and wine, the words of the Bible, the ministering person of the priest, and the entire praying community. Another privileged way of knowing the presence of Christ comes in prayer, and particularly in praying as Jesus did. Jesus prayed in his daily life, in special moments of worship, in the privacy of his heart, and even in times of suffering. In joining our prayer to his we may come to know his presence in a unique way.

### Endnotes

1.  *CCC* 1374: St. Thomas Aquinas, *STh* III, 73, 3c.
2.  "Didache," in *Early Christian Writings*, trans. Maxwell Staniforth (London: Penguin Books, 1968): 231.

## For Reflection

1.  How might the several presences of Christ in the eucharistic action be better explained and related to one another?

2.  Use an example from your own life to illustrate how your prayer approximates the prayer of Jesus.

# CHAPTER 7

# Jesus Christ, Lord of the Future

I n the last half of the twentieth century the teaching of
Christology faced a new and difficult setting that offered
special challenges. The Catholic Church must attempt to
interact positively with an incredible variety of religious views in
modern society. Such a social setting has prompted and almost
forced the Catholic Church to adopt a new attitude toward non-
Christian religious views.

## The Dialogue with Other Religions

This new attitude began officially with the Second Vatican
Council, when bishops from developing countries stressed the
need to re-evaluate the Church's traditionally negative view of
other world religions. In response to their concerns, *Nostra Aetate
(NA)* (Declaration on the Relationship of the Church to Non-
Christian Religions), stated clearly and unambiguously, "The
Catholic Church rejects nothing of what is true and holy in these
religions. She has a high regard for the manner of life and con-
duct, the precepts and doctrines which, although differing in
many ways from her own teaching, nevertheless often reflect a
ray of that truth which enlightens all men" (#2).

With that declaration the Catholic Church initiated a new
appreciation of the positive values within other world religions
and recognized that they possess some genuine teaching about
God and God's plan. This new and official attitude also began an
era of interfaith dialogue aimed at a better understanding of
world religions and nurturing the possibility of communal action
toward major problems in society.

The new attitude of dialogue with other world religions, still in
the process of being shaped, raises a whole new set of questions
about the presentation of Jesus Christ as Son of God, Savior, and
Revealer of God's Plan. These questions emerged more clearly in
the context of official interfaith dialogues initiated after the Second
Vatican Council. In the time prior to the Second Vatican Council,

such issues were scarcely thought of by Catholics. There was only one savior, Jesus Christ; only one religious truth, Catholicism; and no salvation in other religions. "'There is salvation in no one else, for there is no other name under heaven given among mortals by which we must be saved'" (Acts 4:12) stated absolutely what most Catholics believed. Religious teaching about Jesus Christ could, therefore, be established without any other considerations.

> If the Church now recognizes, however, the existence of positive religious values in these other religious traditions, then somehow clear lines of connection to the saving work of Jesus Christ need to be drawn. In the years following the Second Vatican Council, the Catholic Church has continued to develop that initial appreciation in a variety of ways. A 1991 Vatican document summed up the results of twenty-five years of dialogue and study. The Council openly acknowledged the presence of positive values not only in the religious life of individual believers of other religious traditions, but also in the religious traditions to which they belong. It attributed these values to the active presence of God through his Word, pointing also to the universal action of the Spirit. These elements. . . have played and do still play a providential role in the divine economy of salvation.
>
> ("Dialogue and Proclamation," #17)

This document recognizes that salvation and revelation are truly present in other religions and that Catholics need to honor that recognition. A further question, therefore, arises: how are these elements of salvation connected to the salvation effective in Jesus Christ, insofar as these salvific elements usually do not possess any direct connection to the historical Jesus of Nazareth? How might they be connected to Jesus as the Logos, the Son and Word of God? The Catholic Church still endeavors to work out these Christological issues in a satisfactory way. However such resolution happens, it will not negate the ultimate primacy of

Christ's salvation, for *NA* proclaimed, "Yet she proclaims and is in duty bound to proclaim without fail, Christ who is the way, the truth and the life (John 1:6). In him, in whom God reconciled all things to himself (2 Corinthians 5:18–19), men find the fullness of their religious life" (#2).

Therefore, the Church and all its teachers must proclaim Jesus Christ as the Savior of the World, but this proclamation must be done in a fashion that genuinely respects the religious achievements of other religions and their founders. One example of this respect occurred in the 1995 Buddhist-Catholic Agreed Statement which recognized both similarities and differences between the Buddha and Jesus Christ.

> The Buddha is an enlightened human being who shows us the perfection of Buddhahood (perfect selflessness manifested as purity, compassion and wisdom) and gives people the hope that they can themselves attain this ideal. The Buddhahood that can be achieved is a positive condition of human wholeness and freedom characterized by loving kindness, compassion, sympathetic joy and equanimity of affinity, so that one can live fully for the good of others. . . . For Christians, Jesus Christ is the manifestation of God's saving will, the incarnation of the Second Person of the Blessed Trinity, bringing the light of salvation into the world for all humankind once and for all. In the death and resurrection of Jesus Christ, the infinite love and mercy of God that is the source of salvation is also revealed.
>
> (Pontifical Council for Interfaith Dialogue,
> "Buddha and Christ," sec. 4)

Once again, how does a Catholic reconcile the beliefs that other people are offered the possibility of salvation through their own religious traditions and yet proclaim a salvation that comes primarily through Jesus Christ? Although a common solution has been neither worked out in practice nor accepted by the Church's magisterium, several positions to be avoided have been identified.

The first of these alleges that faith in Jesus Christ must be professed and that only those who "explicitly" believe in Jesus Christ can be saved. In the past thirty years, Vatican documents, like the one in 1991 cited earlier, have maintained that the Catholic faith does acknowledge the presence of God's salvation in and through other religions. Therefore, a Hindu is saved by being a good Hindu. The International Theological Commission stated, "Confusion between Christology and theology results if one supposes that the name of God is totally unknown outside of Jesus Christ, and that there exists no other theology than that which arises from the Christian revelation" (*TCA*, #I.A.1.1). All Catholics should be cognizant of these views when they proclaim Jesus Christ as Savior.

A second unacceptable stance professes Jesus as only one of many equal savior figures, a stance that maintains no real uniqueness to Jesus Christ. In this view, all religions are relative, except to their own followers. Such a position has no standing in Catholic Christian theology. The salvation effected by Christ envelops all humanity and all creation, even if Christians today cannot say exactly how that happens. Such an attitude was acknowledged by the Second Vatican Council in one of its most famous statements on this issue.

> All this [joining the Paschal mystery] holds true not for Christians only but also for all men of good will in whose hearts grace is active invisibly. For since Christ died for all, and since all men are in fact called to one and the same destiny, which is divine, we must hold that the Holy Spirit offers to all the possibility of being made partners, *in a way known to God*, in the paschal mystery.
>
> (*GS*, #22; emphasis added)

Catholics must constantly affirm the uniqueness of Christ as Savior and stress the obligation of all believers to preach Jesus Christ as Savior of the World and of all peoples. At the same time, however, they should recognize positive elements of salvation and revelation in other religions as well as the significance of their great religious figures.

With the growth of religious interaction in our country and the world, these kinds of questions about Jesus Christ will surely figure more and more prominently in discussions with both teens and adults. Pastoral ministers will need to blend delicately both principles. One method of doing this might be to connect salvation with the following theme: Jesus Christ as the Lord of the Future.

# Jesus Christ, Lord of the Future

The oldest written document of the New Testament emphasizes that the early Christians believed that the resurrected Jesus would soon return in the fullness of glory. In his First Letter to the Thessalonians, Paul announced that believers were to serve a living and true God and to wait for his Son from heaven, whom he raised from the dead—Jesus, who rescues us from the wrath that is coming (1:9–10).

Similarly, the last words of the New Testament itself are a cry for Jesus to return quickly, "The one who testifies to these things says, 'Surely I am coming soon.' Amen. Come, Lord Jesus!" (Revelation 22:20).

To those first disciples Jesus Christ was not just a figure of the past and a power in the present; he was a hope for the future as well. In his Second Coming, Christ would complete any of his work that remained unfulfilled and bring all things to a glorious conclusion in the mystery of God. "When all things are subjected to him, then the Son himself will also be subjected to the one who put all things in subjection under him, so that God may be all in all" (1 Corinthians 15:28).

But Jesus tarried and did not return in the near future. Some believers from as early as the second generation of Christians were beginning to see that Second Coming only in the far distance, even as they continued to hold to its utter certainty.

> As to the coming of our Lord Jesus Christ and our
> being gathered together to him, we beg you, broth-
> ers and sisters, not to be quickly shaken in mind or

> *alarmed, either by spirit or by word or by letter, as*
> *though from us, to the effect that the day of the Lord*
> *is already here. Let no one deceive you in any way;*
> *for that day will not come unless the rebellion*
> *comes first and the lawless one is revealed.*
>
> (2 Thessalonians 2:1–3)

Still, that future coming remained the moment when all would
be fulfilled and carried out in God's own time. It was simply that,
for the time being, the Church needed to live for the long haul
and take her place in world history.

That belief in Jesus' return (*parousia* in Greek) quickly
became a convergence point for many other related beliefs articulated among the early Christians. These other beliefs included
the resurrection of all the dead; the "Day of the Lord" establishing peace and justice; the end of the world; and the belief in a
final or last judgment that would pass sentence on all the living
and the dead to a state of everlasting blessedness (heaven) or punishment (hell). Christians began to view these events as happening near the time of and along with the future coming of Christ.
Gradually, this integrated vision of the "last things" or the "end
times" became a permanent part of the early Christians' belief
and hope. It would eventually enter into the creeds as a basic
tenet of the Christian faith: "He will come again in glory to judge
the living and the dead." Christians still look to Jesus as the Lord
of the Future, the one who will bring all things to their proper
fulfillment—their individual lives and the universe as a whole.

One of the most important aspects of that future coming
would be Jesus' function as judge of all time and history and
human beings. Jesus and judgment became bound together, cul-
minating a long history of "judgment thinking" in Jewish and
Christian tradition. The judgment of God on the Day of Yahweh
finds its roots in the prophetic tradition of Israel. Amos, Isaiah,
Ezekiel, and Joel all foresaw a special time when God would
intervene in history to pass judgment on Israel and all peoples.

> *The great day of the Lord is near,*
> *near and hastening fast;*

> *the sound of the day of the Lord is bitter,*
> *the warrior cries aloud there.*
> *That day will be a day of wrath,*
> *a day of distress and anguish.*
>
> (Zephaniah 1:14–15)

This judgment would fully enact the covenant, establish justice between peoples, punish the guilty, and save the remaining faithful. Later, in the prophecy of Daniel, the judgment of God was shifted from the present realm of history to the "end of time." Still, there would be judgment, punishment, and, for the faithful, salvation beyond the grave. "Many of those who sleep in the dust of the earth shall awake, some to everlasting life, and some to shame and everlasting contempt" (Daniel 12:2).

All these themes about judgment appear in the teaching of Jesus. The kingdom of God that he proclaimed will involve a divine judgment on all individuals and groups. We are not free to take it or leave it; all people will someday have to answer. The great judgment scene in Matthew's Gospel (see 25:31–46) recounts that all human beings will be called to account before the throne of God; all will be judged by the kindness, mercy, justice, and love they have shown to fellow human beings. "And the king will answer them, 'Truly I tell you, just as you did it to one of the least of these who are members of my family, you did it to me'" (25:40).

It's that simple; not much else matters.

The early Christians handed on this belief in a coming judgment by Jesus Christ as a clear and unambiguous statement of their faith. "For all of us must appear before the judgment seat of Christ, so that each may receive recompense for what has been done in the body, whether good or evil" (2 Corinthians 5:10).

One clarification that they added was quite important; it said that the criteria of God's judgment on human life were reflected in Jesus' life, particularly in his faithfulness all the way to his death. How people follow the example of Jesus determines this judgment. That point then led to a conviction about the overwhelming mercy of God, reflected in the great mercy Jesus himself extended to so many. Disciples were to do their best yet never fail to hope in the overwhelming mercy of God.

> Christ is Lord of eternal life. Full right to pass definitive judgment on the works and hearts of men belongs to him as redeemer of the world. He "acquired" this right by his cross. The Father has given "all judgment to the Son."[1] Yet the Son did not come to judge, but to save and to give the life he has in himself.[2]

Such belief in the value of Jesus' human life became the basis for the Christian belief in the value of every individual human life. What we achieve now through our life "in Christ" will benefit us forever.

> Christians . . . must believe in the fundamental con-tinuity, thanks to the power of the Holy Spirit, between our present life in Christ and the future life [charity is the law of the Kingdom of God and our charity on earth will be the measure of our sharing in God's glory in heaven].
>
> (Congregation for the Doctrine of the Faith, "Letter on Certain Questions Concerning Eschatology," #6)

This conviction of the unqualified value of a "lived life" in God's sight clarifies the position that Christian faith takes against reincarnation. The norm by which we shall be judged is the exemplar of the life of Jesus. Each of us will have to give an account of our lives, according to the example of Jesus. Thus we should always nurture a great hope in the mercy of Christ.

Perhaps now we may reconnect the earlier issue: salvation through Christ and salvation through other religious traditions. Perhaps only at the final fulfillment will our questions about the relationship between Christ and other religions be answered. For the present, the challenge for Catholic Christians is to respect and appreciate other religious traditions even as we continue our own affirmation that Jesus Christ is the ultimate Savior of all creation and humanity and the goal toward which we proceed.

# Summary

The new situation of a society of many religious views has created new challenges for the Catholic faith. The Second Vatican Council has given the directive that Catholics should learn to appreciate the spiritual vision of other world religions. This requires the proclamation of Jesus Christ as the Savior of the world, yet also the recognition of the positive and saving vision of other religious traditions. One way of doing this is to consider Jesus Christ as the Lord of History, the Lord of the Future. In the end of all things, Jesus will reveal exactly how all things have pointed to him as the ultimate fulfillment.

### ENDNOTES

1. *CCC* 679: Jn 5:22; cf. 5:27; *Mt* 25:31; *Acts* 10:42; 17:31; 2 *Tim* 4:1.
2. *CCC* 679: *Jn* 3:17; 5:26.

# For Reflection

1. What are some other religious views that are real and dynamic parts of the worldview of people today? What are some of the positive salvific views these religions offer?

2. What are the norms of judgment that people today see in their image of Christ? How do these correlate with the norms of the Gospel?

# Conclusion

Pope John Paul II strongly indicated that the approach of the millennial year 2000 would afford Christians with an excellent time to renew and enrich their belief in Jesus Christ. For Christians, Jesus stands as the beginning, center, and end of their faith. In words that succinctly recap many of the themes outlined in this booklet, the pope affirms:

> In Jesus Christ the history of salvation finds its culmination and ultimate meaning. In him, we have all received "grace upon grace" (John 1:16), having been reconciled with the Father (cf. Romans 5:10; 2 Corinthians 5:18). . . .The birth of Jesus at Bethlehem is not an event which can be consigned to the past. The whole of human history in fact stands in reference to him: our own time and the future of the world are illumined by his presence. He is "the Living One" (Revelation 1:18), "who is, who was and who is to come" (Revelation 1:4). Before him every knee must bend, in the heavens, on earth and under the earth, and every tongue proclaim that he is Lord (cf. Philippians 2:10–11). In the encounter with Christ, every man discovers the mystery of his own life.
>
> (*Incarnationis Mysterium*
> [The Mystery of the Incarnation], #1)

The joy and grace of knowing Jesus Christ includes many things: the witness of how he has been known and believed in through the Bible; the tradition of the Catholic Church; the dynamism of a living relationship with him in prayer and adoration; and the hope that he will be the fulfillment of all human hopes and history. In this light, Christology becomes truly a great adventure, one that can stimulate and inspire the life of every man, woman, and child.

# ABBREVIATIONS

CCC    *Catechism of the Catholic Church*

DV    *Dei Verbum (Constitution on Divine Revelation)*

GDC    *General Directory for Catechesis*

GS    *Gaudium et Spes (The Pastoral Constitution on the Church in the Modern World)*

NA    *Nostra Aetate (The Declaration on the Church's Relations with non-Christian Religions)*

CF    *The Christian Faith*

SQC    *Select Questions on Christology*

TCA    *Theology Christology Anthropology*

# Bibliography

## Works Cited

Biblical Commission of the Catholic Church. "Sancta Mater
    Ecclesia." In *The Christian Faith: Doctrinal Documents of the
    Catholic Church*, eds. Josef Neuner, SJ, and Jacques Dupuis, SJ.
    5th ed. Staten Island, NY: Alba House, 1990.

Boff, Leonardo. *Jesus the Liberator*. Maryknoll, NY: Orbis Books,
    1978.

Brown, Raymond. *The Birth of the Messiah: A Commentary on the
    Infancy Narratives in Matthew and Luke*. New York: Doubleday
    and Company, 1993.

Bynum, Caroline Walker. *Jesus as Mother: Studies in the Spirituality of
    the High Middle Ages*. Berkeley: University of California Press,
    1982.

*Catechism of the Catholic Church*. Chicago: Loyola Press, 1994.

Christopher, Joseph, ed. and trans. *The Raccolta*. New York: Benziger
    Brothers, Inc., 1952.

Congregation for the Clergy. *General Directory for Catechesis*.
    Washington, DC: United States Catholic Conference, 1998.

Congregation for the Doctrine of the Faith. "Christ, the Trinity and
    Theology Today." *Origins* 1 (March 1990): 666–667.

———. *Instruction on Certain Aspects of the Theology of Liberation*.
    Washington, DC: United States Catholic Conference, 1984.

Council of Trent. "Decree on Justification." In *Decrees of the
    Ecumenical Councils from Nicaea I to Vatican II*, Vol. 2, ed.
    Norman P. Tanner, SJ. Washington, DC: Georgetown University
    Press, 1990.

"Dialogue and Proclamation." *Origins* 21 (July 1991): 125.

"Didache." In *Early Christian Writings*, trans. Maxwell Staniforth. London: Penguin Books, 1968.

*Eucharistic Prayers for Masses with Children and for Masses of Reconciliation*. Washington, DC: United States Catholic Conference, 1975.

Ignatius (bishop of Antioch). "To the Ephesians." In *Early Christian Writings*, trans. Maxwell Staniforth. London: Penguin Books, 1968.

International Commission on English in the Liturgy. *The Sacramentary*. New York: Catholic Book Publishing Company, 1985.

International Theological Commission. *Select Questions on Christology*. Washington, DC: United States Catholic Conference, 1980.

———. *Theology Christology Anthropology*. Washington, DC: United States Catholic Conference, 1983.

"Joint Declaration on the Doctrine of Justification." *Origins* 28 (July 1998): 122.

Neuner, Josef, SJ, and Jacques Dupuis, SJ, eds. *The Christian Faith: Doctrinal Documents of the Catholic Church*. 5th ed. Staten Island, NY: Alba House, 1990.

O'Collins, Gerald. *Christology: A Biblical, Historical and Systematic Study of Jesus*. New York: Oxford University Press, 1995.

Pontifical Council for Interfaith Dialogue. "Buddha and Christ." *Origins* 25 (Sept. 1995): 223.

Pope John Paul II. *Incarnationis Mysterium* (The Mystery of the Incarnation), 1999.

Pope Paul VI. *On Evangelization in the Modern World*. Washington, DC: United States Catholic Conference, 1976.

Saint Athanasius. "Against the Heathen." In *Nicene and Post-Nicene Fathers*. Vol. 4. Grand Rapids, MI: William B. Eerdmans Publishing Company, 1953.

———. "On the Incarnation." In *Athanasius: Contra Gentes and De Incarnatione*, ed. and trans. Robert W. Thomson. Oxford: Clarendon Press, 1971.

Saint Augustine. *Confessions*. Trans. Henry Chadwick. New York: Oxford University Press, 1992.

Saint Justin Martyr. "Apology." In *A New Eusebius: Documents Illustrative of the History of the Church to A.D. 337*, ed. J. Stevenson. London: Society for Promoting Christian Knowledge, 1993.

Second Vatican Council. *Dei Verbum (Dogmatic Constitution on Divine Revelation)*. In *Vatican Council II, Volume 1, Revised Edition: The Conciliar and Post Conciliar Documents*, ed. Austin Flannery, OP, Northport, NY: Costello Publishing Company, 1975.

———. *Gaudium et Spes (Pastoral Constitution on the Church in the Modern World)*. In *Vatican Council II*, Volume 1, Revised Edition: *The Conciliar and Post Conciliar Documents*, ed. Austin Flannery, OP, Northport, NY: Costello Publishing Company, 1975.

———. *Nostra Aetate* (Declaration on the Relations of the Church to Non-Christian Religions). In *Vatican Council II, Volume 1, Revised Edition: The Conciliar and Post Conciliar Documents*, ed. Austin Flannery, OP, Northport, NY: Costello Publishing Company, 1975.

———. *Sacrosanctum Concilium (The Constitution on the Sacred Liturgy)*. In *Vatican Council II, Volume 1, Revised Edition: The Conciliar and Post Conciliar Documents*, ed. Austin Flannery, OP, Northport, NY: Costello Publishing Company, 1975.

Shorter, Aylward. *Toward a Theology of Inculturation*. Maryknoll, NY: Orbis Books, 1988.

Stevenson, J., ed. *A New Eusebius: Documents Illustrative of the History of the Church to A.D. 337*. London: Society for Promoting Christian Knowledge, 1993.

Theological-Historical Commission for the Great Jubilee of the Year 2000. *Jesus Christ, Word of the Father*. New York: Crossroad Publishing Company, 1997.

Ward, Benedicta, trans. *The Prayers and Meditations of Saint Anselm*. New York: Penguin Books, 1973.

# For Further Reading

Barry, William. *Who Do You Say That I Am?* Meeting the Historical Jesus in Prayer. Notre Dame, IN: Ave Maria Press, 1996.

Brown, Raymond. *An Introduction to New Testament Christology.* Mahwah, NJ: Paulist Press, 1995.

Butterworth, G. W., trans. *On First Principles.* Magnolia, MA: Peter Smith, 1991.

Farrelly, John M. *Faith in God Through Jesus Christ.* Collegeville, MN: Liturgical Press, 1997.

Grassi, Joseph. *Rediscovering the Jesus Story.* Mahwah, NJ: Paulist Press, 1995.

Hill, Brennan. *Jesus, the Christ.* Mystic, CN: Twenty-Third Publications, 1994.

Johnson, Elizabeth. *Consider Jesus.* New York: Crossroad Publishing Company, 1990.

Lane, Dermot. *The Reality of Jesus.* Mahwah, NJ: Paulist Press, 1975.

Loewe, William P. *The College Student's Introduction to Christology.* Collegeville, MN: Liturgical Press, 1996.

O'Collins, Gerald, SJ, *Christology: A Biblical, Historical and Systematic Study of Jesus.* New York: Oxford University Press, 1995.

Richard, Lucian. *What Are They Saying About Jesus and World Religions?* Mahwah, NJ: Paulist Press, 1981.

Senior, Donald. *Jesus: A Gospel Portrait,* 2nd ed., rev. Mahwah, NJ.: Paulist Press, 1992.

Sloyan, Gerald. *The Jesus Tradition. Images of Jesus in the West.* Mystic, CN: Twenty-Third Publications, 1986.

# Acknowledgments

The Scripture quotations contained herein are from the New Revised Standard Version Bible, Catholic edition copyright © 1993 and 1989 by the Division of Christian Education of the National Council of the Churches of Christ in the U.S.A. Used by permission. All rights reserved.

English translation of the *Catechism of the Catholic Church for the United States of America* copyright © 1994, United States Catholic Conference, Inc.—Libreria Editrice Vaticana.

Excerpts from the *General Directory for Catechesis* copyright © 1997, United States Catholic Conference, Inc.—Libreria Editrice Vaticana. Used with permission. All rights reserved.

English translation of The Nicene Creed prepared by the English Language Liturgical Commission (ELLC), 1998.

Excerpt from "Against the Heather" in *Nicene and Post-Nicene Fathers*, Series 2, Vol. 4: Athanasius, ed. Philip Schaff and Henry Wace, © 1953, used by permission of Eerdmans Publishing Company. All rights reserved.

Excerpt from *The Birth of the Messiah: A Commentary on the Infancy Narratives in Matthew and Luke* © 1993 by Raymond E. Brown. Reprinted by permission of Doubleday, a division of Random House, Inc. All rights reserved.

Excerpts from *The Christian Faith*, edited by J. Neuner, SJ and J. Dupuis, SJ © 1990 are used by permission of Alba House, a Division of the Society of St. Paul, Staten Island, N.Y. All rights reserved.

Excerpts from *Decrees of the Ecumenical Councils from Nicaea I to Vatican II*, Vol. 2, © 1990 by Norman P. Tanner, SJ, reprinted by permission of Georgetown University Press. All rights reserved.

Excerpts from *Jesus as Mother: Studies in the Spirituality of the High Middle Ages* by Caroline Walker Bynum © 1982 used by permission of The Regents of the University of California, University of California Press, Berkeley. All rights reserved.

Excerpts from *Jesus Christ, Word of the Father*, prepared by the Theological-Historical Commission for the Great Jubilee of the Year 2000, © 1997 used by permission of the Crossroads Publishing Company. All rights reserved.

Excerpts from the *The Raccolta*, ed. and trans. Rev. Joseph Christopher (Benziger Brothers, © 1952) are used by permission of Glencoe/McGraw-Hill. All rights reserved.

# About the Author

Rev. Matthias Neuman, O.S.B., is a monk and priest of Saint Meinrad Archabbey, Saint Meinrad, Indiana. He received his S.T.L. and S.T.D. from the Pontifical University of Saint Anselm in Rome. Father Matthias is senior instructor for theological programs at the Saint Continuing Education Center and chaplain for the Benedictine Sisters of Ferdinand, Indiana. He is a popular speaker who has written over 150 journal articles and reviews dealing with spirituality, ministry, theology, and Benedictine monasticism.